A Glimpse of Paradise

By
Shaykh Mufti Saiful Islām

JKN Publications

© Copyright by JKN Publications

First Published in March 2020

ISBN 978-1-909114-49-4

British Library Cataloguing in Publication Data
A catalogue record for this book is available from the British Library.

All Rights Reserved. No part of this book may be reproduced, stored in a retrieval system, or transmitted in any form or by any means, electronic, mechanical, photocopying, recording or otherwise, without the prior permission of the copyright owner.

Publisher's Note:

Every care and attention has been put into the production of this book. If however, you find any errors they are our own, for which we seek Allāh's ﷻ forgiveness and the reader's pardon.

Published by:

JKN Publications
118 Manningham Lane
Bradford
West Yorkshire
BD8 7JF
United Kingdom

t: +44 (0) 1274 308 456 | w: www.jkn.org.uk | e: info@jkn.org.uk

Book Title: A Glimpse of Paradise

Author: Shaykh Mufti Saiful Islām

Printed by Mega Printing in Turkey

"In the Name of Allāh, the Most Beneficent, the Most Merciful"

Contents

Introduction	6
Sunnah Pertaining to Sūrah Insān	8
Development of a Human	12
Our True Self	12
Reproduction	14
Purpose of Creation	15
Sūrah Ikhlās and Sūrah Kāfirūn	16
Be Grateful to Allāh ﷻ	18
Polish Your Heart with Tawbah	22
Wonders of Jannah	24
Making Promises and Oaths	27
Severity of Qiyāmah	30
Deeds Solely for the Sake of Allāh ﷻ	32
Caring for Allāh's ﷻ Creation	35
Justice of Islām	38
Seeking Allāh's ﷻ Pleasure	39
Virtues of Wudhū	46
Categories of Sabr (Patience)	49
Bounties of Jannah	52
Qur'ān Revealed in Stages	61
Good Company	66
Consultation of the Polytheists	67
Conveying the Message	69
Developing Humility	70

Significance of Dhikr 71
Tahajjud: The Night Prayer 72
Love of the Dunya 75
When Islām Enters the Heart 80
The Qur'ān is a Reminder 83
The Concept of Fate 84
Allāh's ﷻ Mercy 85

Introduction

All praise is due to our Creator and Sustainer; Allāh ﷻ, Lord of the worlds. May peace and blessings be upon our beloved leader and guide, Muhammad ﷺ, his Noble Companions ؓ and his followers till the Last Day. Āmīn.

Mankind has been in existence for only a small fraction of time in comparison to the length of time which has passed prior to our existence, as geological records prove. Even then, the earth did not fail to revolve, despite the fact that we were not present to witness its observation.

Time is the true wealth we have at our disposal though it cannot be amassed. The only way we can utilise it to our advantage is when we do righteous deeds and actions; for this will act in our favour in the Ākhirah (Hereafter). These moments will be preserved in exchange for moments of greater happiness and bliss in the next life and this is the wealth that is enclosed in the constituent we refer to as time. Therefore, we need to perform righteous deeds and actions in the short duration of time we have at our disposal in this transitory worldly life.

We have no covenant or contract guaranteeing the length of time we have in this world. It could range from anything; years, months, days, hours, minutes or even seconds, but one fact of reality which we cannot deny, is that this life will one day come to an end and we will all have to leave the life of this world, far behind.

The period of time measured and allotted to a person is uniquely given to each and every individual according to Allāh's ﷻ infinite knowledge and wisdom. The window of opportunity we have is merely a few moments, to either reap the rewards of gaining eternal salvation, or being condemned to the Hellfire as a result of failing to do so. Time is our wealth that can only be conserved in the form of righteous deeds and actions, otherwise time will only act as a curse resulting in the detriment of our soul.

Sūrah Insān commences with Allāh ﷻ mentioning the period of time when man was not even in existence. This includes the time before the creation of mankind and also the time before a person was sent into this world.

The creation of man and the doomsday connects this Sūrah to the previous Sūrah; Sūrah Qiyāmah.

Sister Alha Begum
February 2020

The Sunnah Pertaining to Sūrah Insān

The Prophet ﷺ would recite this Sūrah every Friday in his Fajr Salāh. Sayyidunā Abū Hurairah ؓ narrated that the Holy Prophet ﷺ used to recite the following in the Fajr prayer of Friday, 'Alif Lām Mīm Tanzīl' (Sūrah As-Sajdah) and 'Hal Atā Alal Insān' (Ad-Dahr)." (Bukhāri)

The reason that the Prophet ﷺ used to recite these particular Sūrahs on this day was to remind the people that just as Allāh ﷻ created Sayyidunā Ādam ؑ on a Friday, the world will also be destroyed on this very day. A common theme in both these Sūrahs is the mention of mankind's creation.

Allāh ﷻ commences Sūrah Insān by mentioning about the origin of man's creation:

$$\text{هَلْ أَتَىٰ عَلَى الْإِنسَانِ حِينٌ مِّنَ الدَّهْرِ لَمْ يَكُن شَيْئًا مَّذْكُورًا}$$

Undoubtedly, a moment in time has passed by man when he was not even something worth mentioning. (76:1)

In the beginning of the Sūrah, the Arabic word 'Hal' is used which means 'Indeed'. The word 'Insān' refers to Sayyidunā Ādam ؑ during the time when Allāh ﷻ intended to create him. After creating Sayyidunā Ādam ؑ, 40 years passed by when he was left between

Makkah and Ṭā'if and thereafter, Allāh ﷻ placed the Rūḥ within him.

The majority of the scholars say that this verse also refers to each and every individual human being before they entered into the realm of this Dunya (world), and this includes the time they spent in the mother's womb. Allāh ﷻ says:

$$\text{خَلَقَكُم مِّن نَّفْسٍ وَاحِدَةٍ ثُمَّ جَعَلَ مِنْهَا زَوْجَهَا وَأَنزَلَ لَكُم مِّنَ الْأَنْعَامِ ثَمَانِيَةَ أَزْوَاجٍ ۚ يَخْلُقُكُمْ فِي بُطُونِ أُمَّهَاتِكُمْ خَلْقًا مِّن بَعْدِ خَلْقٍ فِي ظُلُمَاتٍ ثَلَاثٍ ۚ ذَٰلِكُمُ اللَّهُ رَبُّكُمْ لَهُ الْمُلْكُ ۖ لَا إِلَٰهَ إِلَّا هُوَ ۖ فَأَنَّىٰ تُصْرَفُونَ}$$

He created you from one soul. Then He made from it its mate, and He produced for you from the grazing livestock eight mates. He creates you in the wombs of your mothers, as a creation after a creation in three (layers of) darkness. That is Allāh, your Lord, to Whom all kingdoms belong. There is none worthy of worship but Him so where are you turning to? (39:6)

$$\text{يَا أَيُّهَا النَّاسُ إِن كُنتُمْ فِي رَيْبٍ مِّنَ الْبَعْثِ فَإِنَّا خَلَقْنَاكُم مِّن تُرَابٍ ثُمَّ مِن نُّطْفَةٍ ثُمَّ مِنْ عَلَقَةٍ ثُمَّ مِن مُّضْغَةٍ مُّخَلَّقَةٍ وَغَيْرِ مُخَلَّقَةٍ لِّنُبَيِّنَ لَكُمْ ۚ وَنُقِرُّ فِي الْأَرْحَامِ مَا نَشَاءُ إِلَىٰ أَجَلٍ مُّسَمًّى ثُمَّ نُخْرِجُكُمْ طِفْلًا ثُمَّ لِتَبْلُغُوا أَشُدَّكُمْ ۖ وَمِنكُم مَّن يُتَوَفَّىٰ وَمِنكُم مَّن يُرَدُّ إِلَىٰ}$$

$$\text{أَرْذَلِ الْعُمُرِ لِكَيْلَا يَعْلَمَ مِنْ بَعْدِ عِلْمٍ شَيْئًا ۚ وَتَرَى الْأَرْضَ هَامِدَةً فَإِذَا أَنزَلْنَا عَلَيْهَا الْمَاءَ اهْتَزَّتْ وَرَبَتْ وَأَنبَتَتْ مِن كُلِّ زَوْجٍ بَهِيجٍ}$$

O people! If you are in doubt about Resurrection, then (remember) We have certainly created you from sand, then from a drop of semen, then from a clot of blood, then from a lump of flesh which is shaped (perfectly) or unshaped (deformed) so that We may show you (Our great power). And, according to Our will, We keep you in (your mothers') wombs until an appointed time. Thereafter, We remove you as children, after which you come of age. There are those of you whose souls We claim (at an early age), while others reach the age of infirmity so that they know nothing after once possessing (much) knowledge. And you will see the earth barren, then We send rain to it, causing it to stir, flourish and grow every kind of beautiful species. (22:5)

Two terms which are used to describe man before he came into this world are:
- Wujūd-e-Zāhirī – the point in time when a person was not even present in mind or matter.
- Wujūd-e-Lafẓī – there was no external presence of a person by name.

Before man came into existence, there was no mention of them. Despite this, when a person attains their full strength and maturity, instead of showing gratitude for being alive and in existence, they question the very nature of existence and then go further on in questioning even God's existence.

During the developmental stages in the womb, man did not even have the faculty of intelligence; his senses were in the stages of development, so he was not even aware of his own presence. After he develops and reaches the age of discretion, the faculties which shaped his understanding now become subservient in his eyes. He starts to become more dominant regarding his beliefs and thinks he can conquer his own genetic programming; in his belief of reaching greater intellectual heights.

What he fails to realise is that all the decisions he makes is drawn from the reservoir of his programming which already exists within him and any adjustment he makes is also regulated accordingly from within.

The innate conscience always draws us back when we stray but becomes subdued when a person's evil deeds reach critical levels overriding the conscience. This is when man feels that he has become intellectually invincible. At this stage, his intrinsic pathway to God's calling becomes barricaded and shut down.

This is when man becomes audacious. He forgets his own beginning of non-existence to the extent that he then questions everything in existence, all the way up until he questions the very existence of God.

Mankind should take lessons from his bad behaviour. When man holds his conscience in contempt by indulging in evil deeds and actions, then fallacious ideologies become readily embraced and accepted by him.

Development of a Human

After conception, the embryo develops into a foetus. At the stage of four months, the Rūh is placed within the developing foetus. At this time, four things are determined:
- A person's A'māl (deeds).
- A person's Rizq (sustenance).
- When a person's life will end.
- Whether the person will be fortunate or unfortunate.

When we attain the stage of adulthood, the worry of earning our livelihood plagues our mind to the extent that we forget about our real sense of purpose and existence.

Our True Self

Mutarif ؓ; a pious predecessor once saw a youngster walking very haughtily; puffed up with arrogance and pride. He approached him and said, "O my son, don't walk like this."

The youngster turned to him and said, "Do you know who I am?" Mutarrif ؒ replied, "I know exactly who you are! Your beginning was that you were an impure semen, your ending is that you will be a decomposed body and in-between you are carrying waste in your body."

If we take a moment to ponder, we will realise that this is the true reality of each and every single individual.
Allāh ﷻ says:

$$\text{اَللّٰهُ الَّذِيْ خَلَقَكُمْ مِّنْ ضَعْفٍ ثُمَّ جَعَلَ مِنْ بَعْدِ ضَعْفٍ قُوَّةً ثُمَّ جَعَلَ مِنْ بَعْدِ قُوَّةٍ ضَعْفًا وَّشَيْبَةً ۚ يَخْلُقُ مَا يَشَاءُ ۚ وَهُوَ الْعَلِيْمُ الْقَدِيْرُ}$$

It is Allāh Who created you in a state of weakness, then substituted strength after the weakness and, after the strength, will again give weakness and old-age. Allāh creates whatever He wills and He is the All-Knowing, All-Powerful. (30:54)

This is why Khwājah Azīzul Hasan Majzūb ؒ says, "In childhood you ate and drank without a care in the world. When you reached your youthhood, you became insane, and in old age you were stricken with ailments, and then when life comes to an end, everything ceased. This world is not a place for amusement but a place to take a lesson from."

Reproduction

Allāh ﷻ uses the Arabic word 'Amshāj' to describe the mixture of male and female discharge. The father's sperm and the mother's ovum fuse together during fertilisation to produce an embryo which eventually grows into a human being. 1400 years ago, the fusing of the male sperm with the female ovum was not in any way known, but Allāh ﷻ mentions the process of reproduction.
Allāh ﷻ says:

إِنَّا خَلَقْنَا الْإِنْسَانَ مِنْ نُطْفَةٍ أَمْشَاجٍ نَبْتَلِيهِ فَجَعَلْنَاهُ سَمِيعًا بَصِيرًا

Indeed We have created man from a mixed seed to test him and We made him hearing and seeing. (76:2)

When a person analyses the verses mentioning about reproduction in the Holy Qur'ān, the question arises as to how the Holy Prophet ﷺ could have known about all the different stages of a developing embryo. To think that the Holy Prophet ﷺ, who was unlettered, could have had knowledge of all the different stages of reproduction sounds implausible unless there was a divine presence that was guiding him with this knowledge.

Intelligence also has its limitations, as a person wouldn't know *all* the answers to their questions without a link to an external greater power. This is where divine revelation comes, to lead man from the shadows of darkness into light. Through the Prophet ﷺ, Allāh ﷻ has shown us the path of guidance.

Purpose of Creation

Allāh ﷻ uses the Arabic word 'Nabtalīhi' in this verse, which refers to the fact that man will be tested. This worldly life is a test and it is the very reason why we were created in the first instance. This is why Allāh ﷻ says in the Qur'ān:

$$\text{وَمَا خَلَقْتُ الْجِنَّ وَالْإِنْسَ إِلَّا لِيَعْبُدُونِ}$$

I have created man and Jinn only to worship Me. (51:56)

In another place Allāh ﷻ states:

$$\text{اَلَّذِيْ خَلَقَ الْمَوْتَ وَالْحَيَاةَ لِيَبْلُوَكُمْ أَيُّكُمْ أَحْسَنُ عَمَلًا ۚ وَهُوَ الْعَزِيْزُ الْغَفُوْرُ}$$

He has created death and life to test which of you carry out the best acts. He is the Mighty, the Most Forgiving. (67:2)

When we wake up in the morning, we are instructed to begin our day by reciting the following Masnūn Du'ā:

$$\text{اَلْحَمْدُ لِلّٰهِ الَّذِيْ أَحْيَانَا بَعْدَ مَا أَمَاتَنَا وَإِلَيْهِ النُّشُوْرُ}$$

(All praise be to Allāh ﷻ Who gave us life after death and to Him we will be raised and returned)

Sūrah Ikhlās and Sūrah Kāfirūn

After having woken up, we are required to perform the Fajr Salāh before sunrise. In the first two Rak'āt of this Salāh, it is Sunnah to recite Sūrah Kāfirūn in the first Rak'āt and Sūrah Ikhlās in the second Rak'āt:

قُلْ يَٰٓأَيُّهَا ٱلْكَٰفِرُونَ ۝ لَآ أَعْبُدُ مَا تَعْبُدُونَ ۝ وَلَآ أَنتُمْ عَٰبِدُونَ مَآ أَعْبُدُ ۝ وَلَآ أَنَا۠ عَابِدٌ مَّا عَبَدتُّمْ ۝ وَلَآ أَنتُمْ عَٰبِدُونَ مَآ أَعْبُدُ ۝ لَكُمْ دِينُكُمْ وَلِيَ دِينِ ۝

Say, 'O disbelievers! I do not worship what you worship nor do you worship what I worship. I am neither a worshipper of that which you worship nor are you worshippers of that which I worship. For you is your religion and for me is mine.' (1-6)

When a person recites Sūrah Kāfirūn, they begin by negating Kufr (disbelief). In beginning the prayer, we seek refuge from Shaytān and then when a person recites the Basmalah (Tasmiyah), they are placing Allāh's ﷻ Sifāt (attributes) within themselves. By following the second Rak'at with the recital of Sūrah Ikhlās, we begin the day in reminding ourselves of Allāh's ﷻ oneness and uniqueness of His eternal qualities in allowing us to commence our day enveloped in its beauty. We reaffirm our faith by first cleansing our heart from

Kufr, and then recapitulating the beauty of Allāh's ﷻ oneness into our hearts by the recital of Sūrah Ikhlās.

$$\text{قُلْ هُوَ اللّٰهُ أَحَدٌ ۞ اَللّٰهُ الصَّمَدُ ۞ لَمْ يَلِدْ وَلَمْ يُولَدْ ۞ وَلَمْ يَكُنْ لَّهُ كُفُوًا أَحَدٌ ۞}$$

Say, 'He Allāh is One. Allāh is Independent. He has no children and is not anyone's child. There is none equal to Him.'

(112:1-4)

At the end of the day, after the Fardh of Maghrib Salāh in our 2 Rak'at of Sunnah, we are also taught to recite these two Sūrahs in the same order in negating Kufr once again and adorning ourselves with the light of Allāh's ﷻ oneness.

As the darkness of the night enfolds upon us and draws in, we mark the ending of our prayers by reciting Sūrah A'lā in the first Rak'at of the Witr prayer, followed by the same repetition of Sūrah Kāfirūn and Sūrah Ikhlās in the second and third Rak'at respectively.

The Kirāman Kātibīn are the Angels who are assigned to record every individual deed; good and bad. We have been given the Hawās-e-Khamsa - the five senses which give us the ability to:
1. See
2. Hear
3. Taste
4. Touch
5. Smell

These senses enable us to make sense of the world around us. The next adaptation which follows on from this is that of intellect, which assists us in understanding things to a greater degree and depth which is obtained by our senses. This is the distinguishing line which differentiates us from all the other animals.

Allāh ﷻ says:

$$ لَقَدْ خَلَقْنَا الْإِنْسَانَ فِي أَحْسَنِ تَقْوِيمٍ $$

Undoubtedly, We created man in the best form. (95:4)

Be Grateful to Allāh ﷻ

$$ إِنَّا هَدَيْنَاهُ السَّبِيلَ إِمَّا شَاكِرًا وَإِمَّا كَفُورًا $$

We guided him to the path so he is either grateful or ungrateful. (76:3)

In this verse, two Arabic words have been used, Shākir (grateful) and Kafūr (ungrateful). The word Shākir is Isme Fā'il (active participle) whereas the word Kafūr is Isme Mubālaga (shows intensity in meaning), i.e. it refers to a large amount.

Scholars mention that there are few who are grateful and the majority are ungrateful, so the Arabic word Shākir conveys the meaning of those few who are grateful.

Many a times, the evil deeds may seem alluring, but the good and evil can never be equal. Allāh ﷻ says:

$$\text{قُل لَّا يَسْتَوِي الْخَبِيثُ وَالطَّيِّبُ وَلَوْ أَعْجَبَكَ كَثْرَةُ الْخَبِيثِ ۚ فَاتَّقُوا اللَّهَ يَا أُولِي الْأَلْبَابِ لَعَلَّكُمْ تُفْلِحُونَ}$$

Say, 'The impure and pure are not equal even though the abundance of the impure may attract you. So fear Allāh, O people of intelligence that you may be successful.' (5:100)

In this life, there will be more people who disbelieve than believe and there will be more things forbidden than permissible.

Once Sayyidunā Umar al-Fārūq ؓ was walking past a person and overheard him supplicating the following Du'ā, "O Allāh make me from among those who are few." Sayyidunā Umar al-Fārūq ؓ had never come across such a Du'ā before so he enquired about this Du'ā asking, "Brother, what kind of Du'ā are you making?" The man replied, "Have you not read the following verse?"

$$\text{اِعْمَلُوا آلَ دَاوُودَ شُكْرًا ۚ وَقَلِيلٌ مِّنْ عِبَادِيَ الشَّكُورُ}$$

"Work, O family of Dāwūd! Express your thanks." Few of My servants are grateful. (34:13)

Sayyidunā Umar al-Fārūq ؓ upon hearing this, wept and admonished himself saying, "The people are more knowledgeable than you, O Umar! O Allāh ﷻ, make us of your 'few' servants."

In another verse Allāh ﷻ says regarding those who will enter Jannah (Paradise):

$$\text{فِي جَنَّاتِ النَّعِيمِ ۞ ثُلَّةٌ مِّنَ الْأَوَّلِيْنَ ۞ وَقَلِيْلٌ مِّنَ الْآخِرِيْنَ ۞}$$

They will be in Jannat of bliss. A large group from among the earlier ones and a few from among the later ones. (56:12–14)

The Arabic word 'Qalīl' (few) has also been used in this verse denoting that a small amount of people will enter into Jannah.

In another verse Allāh ﷻ says:

$$\text{مَّا يَفْعَلُ اللهُ بِعَذَابِكُمْ إِنْ شَكَرْتُمْ وَآمَنْتُمْ ۚ وَكَانَ اللهُ شَاكِرًا عَلِيْمًا}$$

What must Allāh punish you for if you are grateful and have Īmān. Allāh is Most Appreciative, All-Knowing. (4:147)

The two qualities that Allāh ﷻ expects from us is that we are believers and that we are grateful. In matters of Dīn, we should look to those above us in knowledge and virtue so that we are inspired to emulate them, but when it comes to worldly matters, we should look to those who have less than ourselves so that we do not belittle the blessings that Allāh ﷻ has bestowed upon us.

Sayyidunā Abū Hurairah ؓ reported that the Messenger of Allāh ﷺ said: "If one of you looks at those who are blessed over him in wealth and appearance, let him look at those below him." In another narration the Holy Prophet ﷺ said: "Do not look at those above you, lest you view the favours of Allāh ﷻ trivial." (Bukhārī)

And we see the difficulties and hardship that people are facing across the world, with millions deprived of even the bare necessities.

$$إِنَّا هَدَيْنَاهُ السَّبِيلَ إِمَّا شَاكِرًا وَّإِمَّا كَفُورًا$$

We guided him to the path so he is either grateful or ungrateful. (76:3)

This refers to being grateful in recognising the Creator and for all the blessings and bounties, or showing ingratitude in rejecting Allāh ﷻ and being averse to His orders and commands. This is why Allāh ﷻ says:

$$وَهَدَيْنَاهُ النَّجْدَيْنِ$$

... and showed him the two paths (of right and wrong so that he may choose which path he wishes to follow). (90:10)

Imām Abū Hanīfah ﷺ says that the intellect is such, that if no guidance came to a person, they would still be obliged to believe in the oneness of Allāh ﷻ. It would be derived from their own intelligence, which is totally natural. If there remained any place in the world where the message had not reached, then belief in this alone would be sufficient in achieving salvation.

For every tribe and nation, Allāh ﷻ sent a Prophet to remind the people of the straight path, which would lead to salvation and success in the afterlife. A person is born with the natural inclination to recognise virtue over evil but when a person continuously commits sins, this recognition diminishes.

Polish Your Heart with Tawbah (Repentance)

Sayyidunā Abū Hurairah ﷺ reports that the Messenger of Allāh ﷺ said, "Verily when the servant commits a sin, a black mark appears upon his heart. If he abandons the sin, seeks forgiveness and repents then his heart will be polished. If he returns to the sin, the blackness will be increased until it overcomes his heart. (Tirmizi)

It is the covering that Allāh ﷻ has mentioned:

كَلَّا ۖ بَلْ ۜ رَانَ عَلَىٰ قُلُوبِهِم مَّا كَانُوا يَكْسِبُونَ

No, rather a covering is over their hearts from what they have earned. (83:14)

In another verse Allāh ﷻ says:

$$\text{خَتَمَ اللّٰهُ عَلٰى قُلُوْبِهِمْ وَعَلٰى سَمْعِهِمْ ۖ وَعَلٰۤى أَبْصَارِهِمْ غِشَاوَةٌ ۖ وَّلَهُمْ عَذَابٌ عَظِيْمٌ}$$

Allāh has placed a seal upon their hearts and upon their hearing, while there is a veil over their eyes. Theirs shall be a terrible punishment. (2:7)

$$\text{أَفَلَمْ يَسِيْرُوْا فِى الْأَرْضِ فَتَكُوْنَ لَهُمْ قُلُوْبٌ يَّعْقِلُوْنَ بِهَاۤ أَوْ آذَانٌ يَّسْمَعُوْنَ بِهَا ۖ فَإِنَّهَا لَا تَعْمَى الْأَبْصَارُ وَلٰكِنْ تَعْمَى الْقُلُوْبُ الَّتِيْ فِى الصُّدُوْرِ}$$

So have they not travelled through the earth and have hearts by which to reason and ears by which to hear? For indeed, it is really not the eyes that become blind, but it is the hearts that lie in the bosoms which become blind. (22:46)

$$\text{إِنَّاۤ أَعْتَدْنَا لِلْكَافِرِيْنَ سَلَاسِلَ وَأَغْلَالًا وَّسَعِيْرًا}$$

Verily for the disbelievers We have prepared chains, yokes (fetters) and a flaming fire. (76:4)

The disbelievers will be restrained in fetters, unable to move. They won't be successful in finding even the slightest relief, as they are made to suffer the torment of the Hellfire.

Wonders of Jannah

$$\text{إِنَّ ٱلْأَبْرَارَ يَشْرَبُونَ مِن كَأْسٍ كَانَ مِزَاجُهَا كَافُورًا ۞ عَيْنًا يَشْرَبُ بِهَا عِبَادُ ٱللَّهِ يُفَجِّرُونَهَا تَفْجِيرًا ۞}$$

The righteous shall certainly drink from a cup which contains a mixture of Kāfūr (camphor), A spring from which Allāh's bondsmen shall drink and which they shall cause to flow abundantly. (76:5-6)

Allāh ﷻ says that the people of Jannah will cause a fountain or a spring to gush forth, as all these things will be under their authority. This will not be like in the world where a person borrows something, or gets it on rent for a certain length of time; it will be theirs forever. It will be given as Mīrāth (inheritance) as a result of the good deeds that they carried out in the life of this world.

Allāh ﷻ says:

$$\text{وَلَقَدْ كَتَبْنَا فِي ٱلزَّبُورِ مِن بَعْدِ ٱلذِّكْرِ أَنَّ ٱلْأَرْضَ يَرِثُهَا عِبَادِيَ ٱلصَّالِحُونَ}$$

Without doubt, We have already written in the Zabūr after the reminder that My pious bondsmen shall inherit the land (of Jannah). (21:105)

The Arabic word which Allāh ﷻ uses for inheritance is 'Mīrāth'. The question arises as to why Allāh ﷻ says that the believers shall inherit

Jannah instead of being given Jannah. To understand this, first we must understand the conditions of inheritance, which are as follows:
- The heir is given a fixed share.
- It is given at an appointed time.

When a person dies, a fixed share is given to the heirs of the deceased as their right of inheritance. Similarly, Jannah is the fixed share of which Allāh ﷻ will give to the believers as it becomes their right owing to their good deeds. Just as inheritance is given to a person at the death of their kin; after the deceased has been buried and the legal costs and debts have been settled; similarly, it is only when a person dies that they are also given Jannah after the interim period is over – the Day of Judgement; when the debts of virtue and vice are settled.

Sayyidunā Abdullāh Ibn Abbās ؓ says, that the names of some of the food and drink in Jannah have been mentioned so that we can imagine the likeness of the food that we will be given, but the taste will stand in no comparison to the taste of the food and drink in Jannah.

The fruits of Jannah will have 70 different colours and tastes, so although they may resemble the fruits of the earth in likeness, the taste of the fruits will be unlike anything that a person has ever experienced. For example, it mentions in a Hadīth:

The Messenger of Allāh ﷺ reports that Allāh ﷻ said, '**I have prepared for My righteous slaves in Paradise what no eyes has ever seen, no ears have ever heard of and what has never come to the heart and mind of a human being; recite if you wish: And no soul knows what has been hidden for them for the comfort of the eyes i.e. (satisfaction) as reward for what they used to do. (32:17)**' (Bukhārī and Muslim)

In Paradise there will be two categories of people:
1. The Abrār – the righteous people.
2. The Muqarrabūn – those who will be very close to Allāh ﷻ, these people will be on a higher level of Jannah.

A person will receive the comforts of Jannah according to the level they attain. The Abrār are the people who will be given their book of deeds in their right hand. These people will be able to direct the water fountains in whichever direction they wish. This water will be mixed with camphor which will further enhance the taste. Why is this given to the righteous people? One of the reasons is because they used to fulfil their vows. Thus, if we make a promise, we too need to ensure that we fulfil these pledges.

Making Promises and Oaths

Sayyidunā Abdullāh ؓ narrates that the Prophet ﷺ said: "The best people are those of my generation, and then those who will come after them (the next generation), and then those who will come after them (i.e. the next generation). And then after them, there will come people whose witness will proceed their oaths and whose oaths will proceed their witness." (Bukhāri)

Sayyidunā Abū Hurairah ؓ reports that the Messenger of Allāh ﷺ said: "Do not make vows, for vows do not change Qadr (the divine decree) but they make the stingy person give something up." (Muslim)

This is why the Prophet ﷺ would tell the people to refrain from making vows saying that it does not avert anything, but only draws from the miser. For example, there are those who refrain from spending their wealth in the path of Allāh ﷻ but then make a pledge with Allāh ﷻ that if they pass a certain test or exam, they will give. Then, many a times when Allāh ﷻ fulfils their wishes, a person becomes miserly in giving or fails to give at all, when in fact we should be giving anyhow, regardless of the situation we find ourselves in.

There was an individual whose son was very ill. He came into the Masjid and supplicated, "O Allāh, if you return my son back to health I will donate a cow." He returned home to see his son feeling slightly better. He then went back to the Masjid feeling that giving a cow was going to be too costly. He amended his Du'ā, saying, "O

Allāh, if you return my son back to health I will give a goat instead." After returning home once again, he found his son's condition even further improved. He then felt that giving a goat was going to be extortionate so he returned back to the Masjid and prayed once again, this time saying, "O Allāh, if you return my son back to health I will give a chicken instead." He returned home once more to find his son had completely recovered so he returned back to the Masjid and prayed, "O Allāh, this time I will leave it and next time I will give it instead."

A believer should always be open-handed and generous, and not wait until they are stricken by a calamity before deciding to give in the path of Allāh ﷻ. And there are some that even though they promise to give something, they do not keep their word once the outcome is in their favour, of Allāh ﷻ fulfilling their Du'ās, as the above example illustrates.

A man who made a vow that he would do 100,000 Tawāf if Allāh ﷻ fulfilled his wish. Subsequently, Allāh ﷻ fulfilled his wish and now this man is performing Tawāf day and night in order to fulfil his vow. We should not make such extreme oaths or any oaths for that matter, but when a person feels compelled for any reason, they should give serious thought to the oaths they make because many people are in the habit of swearing oaths which then become impossible to fulfil.

Sayyidunā Abdullāh Ibn Umar ؓ says that his father Sayyidunā Umar al-Farūq ؓ went to the Prophet ﷺ and said, "I made a vow during the time of Jāhilīyyah (ignorance) that I would do I'tikāf in

Masjid Al-Harām. The Prophet ﷺ said to Sayyidunā Umar al-Fārūq ؓ, "Then fulfil your vow."

Even when a person makes a vow, there are conditions:
- A person can only make vows on things that they personally own and want to give, *not* on another person's belongings. For example, a person cannot say things such as, "If I pass my driving test, I will give my friend's car away in the path of Allāh ﷻ." This vow will be null and void because the person is not the owner of their friend's car.
- A person cannot make a vow on something that is already compulsory. For example a person cannot say, "If I pass my exam, then I will read Fajr Salāh," as the Salāh is already compulsory on the person in the first instance.
- A person can only make a vow on those things which are permissible. For example, a person makes a vow that they are going to perform I'tikāf. This type of oath would be within the limits of permissibility.

$$ يُوفُونَ بِالنَّذْرِ وَيَخَافُونَ يَوْمًا كَانَ شَرُّهُ مُسْتَطِيرًا $$

They fulfil their vows and fear the Day (of Judgement), the difficulty of which shall be widespread. (76:7)

Severity of Qiyāmah

Once the Holy Prophet ﷺ came to the chamber of Sayyidah Ā'ishah ؓ and found her crying upon hearing this verse. The Prophet ﷺ then said that there would arise three occasions where no one will remember anyone:

1. When the Book of Deeds will be presented to a person – the sheer worry on that Day will make a person forget about everything else.
2. At the time when a person's deeds will be weighed.
3. When a person is about to cross the Sirāt (bridge).

On this Day, the situation will be so severe that some people will be drowning in their own sweat, as mentioned in the following Hadīth. The Prophet ﷺ said: "The sun will come very close to the creation on the Day of Judgement until it will be like one mile from them. People will then drown according to the extent of their actions. From among them there will be those who will be in their sweat up to their ankles. Others, their sweat will be up to their knees. Some will be in sweat up to their waists, and others will be in their sweat up to their mouths." (Muslim)

In another verse Allāh ﷻ says:

فَإِذَا جَاءَتِ الصَّاخَّةُ ۞ يَوْمَ يَفِرُّ الْمَرْءُ مِنْ أَخِيهِ ۞ وَأُمِّهِ وَأَبِيهِ ۞ وَصَاحِبَتِهِ وَبَنِيهِ ۞ لِكُلِّ امْرِئٍ مِنْهُمْ يَوْمَئِذٍ شَأْنٌ يُغْنِيهِ ۞

So when the deafening scream (the sound of the Trumpet) will come...on that Day man will run from his brother, his mother, his father, his wife and his sons. On that Day every one of them will be preoccupied with a predicament that will make him oblivious of another. (80:33–37)

In a Hadīth related by Sayyidah Ā'ishah ﷺ the Holy Prophet ﷺ said: "The people will be assembled barefoot, naked and uncircumcised." I said, "O Messenger of Allāh, will the men and women look at each other?" The Prophet ﷺ said, "The matter will be too serious for them to notice." (Bukhārī and Muslim)

Deeds Solely for the Sake of Allāh ﷻ

$$\text{وَيُطْعِمُونَ الطَّعَامَ عَلٰى حُبِّهٖ مِسْكِيْنًا وَّيَتِيْمًا وَّأَسِيْرًا ۞ إِنَّمَا نُطْعِمُكُمْ لِوَجْهِ اللهِ لَا نُرِيْدُ مِنْكُمْ جَزَاءً وَّلَا شُكُوْرًا ۞}$$

Out of love for Allāh, they feed the poor, the orphan and the captive (saying), 'We feed you only for Allāh's pleasure and desire neither a return nor thanks from you.' (76:8-9)

This verse was revealed after the following incident took place. One day, Sayyidunā Ali ؓ came home to find that there was no food available. He met a Jewish man and asked him if he could borrow some money. The man declined. He then asked if he could work for him for that day in order to earn some money; the man agreed. He did all the jobs that were needed doing such as drawing water out from the well and all the rest of the work that was expected from him. The Jewish man then gave him some wheat. He took this home and then proceeded to make three flatbreads for himself and his two children; Sayyidunā Hasan ؓ and Sayyidunā Husain ؓ.

As he was about to give the first flatbread to his children, a Miskīn (poor person) came by, so instead of feeding it to his children, he gave it to the Miskīn. He then got the second flatbread ready and was about to give it to his children when an orphan knocked at the door. Sayyidunā Ali ؓ then took the flatbread and gave it to the orphan.

After finishing making the last flatbread, he once again proceeded to give it to his children but this time, a captive stood waiting at the door. He then gave his last flatbread to the captive and he and his family stayed hungry that night.

Subhān-Allāh! The love the Sahābah ؓ had for the poor and the needy was such that they would prefer them over themselves and their families.

Sayyidunā Abū Hurairah ؓ reported: A man came to the Prophet ﷺ and said: "O Messenger of Allāh ﷺ, which charity has the greatest reward?" The Prophet ﷺ said, "That you give charity while you are healthy, feeling greedy, fearing poverty and hoping to get rich. Do not delay giving until you are on your deathbed, then say, 'Give to such a person. It already belongs to that person.'" (Bukhārī and Muslim)

Sayyidunā Abdullāh Ibn Umar ؓ narrates, A man asked the Prophet ﷺ: "Which Islām is good or what sort of deeds (or what qualities of) Islām are good?" The Prophet ﷺ replied, "To feed (others) and to greet those whom you know and those whom you do not know." (Bukhārī)

In another verse Allāh ﷻ says:

$$\text{وَيُؤْثِرُونَ عَلَىٰ أَنْفُسِهِمْ وَلَوْ كَانَ بِهِمْ خَصَاصَةٌ ۚ وَمَنْ يُوقَ شُحَّ نَفْسِهِ فَأُولَٰئِكَ هُمُ الْمُفْلِحُونَ}$$

They prefer (others) above themselves even though they are themselves in need. Those who are saved from the miserliness of the soul are really the successful ones. (59:9)

$$\text{لَنْ تَنَالُوا الْبِرَّ حَتَّىٰ تُنْفِقُوا مِمَّا تُحِبُّونَ ۚ وَمَا تُنْفِقُوا مِنْ شَيْءٍ فَإِنَّ اللَّهَ بِهِ عَلِيمٌ}$$

You shall never reach (perfect) righteousness until you spend out of that which you love. Whatever good you spend, Allāh is certainly Aware of it. (3:92)

When this verse was revealed, the Sahābah Kirām ﷺ would always try to grasp every opportunity they could in spending in the path of Allāh ﷻ.

Sayyidunā Abū Talhah ﷺ was one such Sahābi. He had a huge orchard, and when this verse was revealed, he came and donated this entire orchard as it was his most prized possession. He asked the Prophet ﷺ to spend it wherever he deemed it fit. The Prophet ﷺ then distributed it amongst Sayyidunā Abū Talhah's ﷺ relatives so that he would gain a two fold reward – one would be of Sadaqah and the other was fulfilling the rights of kith and kin by being generous towards them. This is a far cry from what we witness nowadays unfortunately – people only want to give those things which are of no use to them and are of inferior quality.

Allāh ﷻ says in the Qur'ān:

$$\text{يَا أَيُّهَا الَّذِينَ آمَنُوا أَنْفِقُوا مِنْ طَيِّبَاتِ مَا كَسَبْتُمْ وَمِمَّا أَخْرَجْنَا لَكُمْ مِنَ الْأَرْضِ ۖ وَلَا تَيَمَّمُوا الْخَبِيثَ مِنْهُ تُنْفِقُونَ وَلَسْتُمْ بِآخِذِيهِ إِلَّا أَنْ تُغْمِضُوا فِيهِ ۚ وَاعْلَمُوا أَنَّ اللَّهَ غَنِيٌّ حَمِيدٌ}$$

O you who have Īmān! Spend of the pure things that you have earned and of that which We reproduce for you from the earth. Do not intend (to spend in charity) the inferior things which you would not yourselves take except with closed eyes. Know that verily Allāh is Independent, Worthy of praise. (2:267)

Caring for Allāh's ﷻ Creation

The Prophet ﷺ said that even feeding animals is a commendable act and this will also be rewarded as mentioned in the following Hadīth: Sayyidunā Surāqah Ibn Ju'shum ؓ reported: I asked the Messenger of Allāh ﷺ about a lost camel who comes to drink from my cisterns that I have prepared for my own camels, "Will I be rewarded if I give it some water to drink?" The Prophet ﷺ said, "In every living being is a reward for charity." (Ibn Mājah)

Sayyidunā Abū Hurairah ؓ reports that the Messenger of Allāh ﷺ said: "While a man was walking, on his way he became extremely thirsty. He found a well. He went down into it to drink some water. Upon leaving it, he saw a dog which was panting out of thirst. His tongue was lolling out and he was eating moist earth due to extreme thirst. He thought to himself, 'This dog is extremely thirsty as I was.' So he descended into the well, filled up his leather sock with water and holding it in his teeth, climbed up and quenched the thirst of the dog. Allāh ﷻ appreciated his action and forgave his sins." The Companions ؓ asked, "Will we be rewarded for showing the animals kindness also?" The Prophet ﷺ said, "A reward is given in connection with every living creature." (Bukhāri and Muslim) A similar Hadīth is also narrated about a prostitute who was also forgiven as a result of giving a thirsty dog water to drink.

When a person provides food for another person, this is an act of great virtue as mentioned in the following Hadīth: Sayyidunā Abdullāh Ibn Salām ؓ reports from the Messenger of Allāh ﷺ who said: "O people, spread Salām, feed the hungry, maintain relationships and pray at night when people are sleeping and you will enter Paradise in peace." (Tirmizi)

In another Hadīth it says regarding feeding those in need: Sayyidunā Abū Hurairah ؓ reported that the Messenger of Allāh ﷺ said: "The poor man (Miskīn) is not the person who goes round to the people and is dismissed with one or two morsels and one or two dates." They (the Companions of the Prophet ﷺ) enquired, "Messenger of Allāh ﷺ, then who is a Miskīn?" He replied, "He who does not get enough to satisfy him and he is not considered so (as to elicit the attention of the benevolent people), so that charity may be given to him, and he does not beg anything from people." (Muslim)

Subhān-Allāh, every act of kindness is rewarded, even to the extent of showing kindness to animals. In this day and age, this is seen to be expected of any moral individual but if we take a step back in history, we realise that animals were only given rights just over 150 years ago. Prior to this time, this concept was unheard of in the western world.

Imagine how it would have come across over 1400 years ago when the Prophet ﷺ gave rights to animals saying the you could not overburden them nor overwork them, and also said that a person would be held accountable for any cruelty meted out to an animal. The Prophet ﷺ also gave an example of a woman who had tied her cat and on account of being restrained, could not go out looking for food and as a result died of hunger; saying she would enter Hellfire on account of this evil deed alone.

Another example is given as follows:

A group of Companions ﷺ were once on a journey with the Prophet ﷺ and he left them for a while. During his absence, they saw a bird with its two young chicks and they took the young ones from the nest. The mother bird was circling above in the air, beating its wings in grief, when the Prophet ﷺ came back. He said: "Who has hurt the feelings of this bird by taking its children? Return them to her." (Muslim)

If this is the Akhlāq that a person is to show to animals, then how much more important would it be to show compassion and regard to our fellow human beings.

Justice of Islām

For those who take the Qur'anic verses out of context and say that Islām is a religion that promotes violence against other human beings – how can this be substantiated? The Holy Prophet ﷺ not only gave rights to individuals, but rights to even animals; something which was unprecedented at the time. It was only recently acknowledged and integrated after being enforced by law, less than 200 years ago.

Even when people were divided into classes and hierarchy, the lowest being that of the ranks of slaves, even then the Prophet ﷺ reminded the people that in the sight of Allāh ﷻ, a person's status was on account of how much Taqwa (God consciousness) a person had and not according to their lineage and social status. As slavery was so deeply ingrained in society, immediate abolishment would have caused anarchy and turmoil in a society which was already undergoing transformation and change from the practice of idolatry to Tawhīd.

A gradual abolishment of slavery was set in motion by the Prophet ﷺ on account of the delicate and fragile conditions that existed during this period. This however, did not prevent slaves from excelling;

many went on to become some of the greatest learned people and jurists of all time, with people flocking to them in droves in order to benefit from their knowledge.

Islām had channelled a new pathway which did not impose limitations on a person succeeding and excelling when it came to learning and rising in rank as a result of this knowledge. The knowledge of Dīn was seen as the essential ingredient that caused a person to be elevated in rank and position, regardless of their social class or the background they had originated from.

The transformation that we have seen only recently in the last few decades or so, with societies still struggling with integration – many lessons are yet to be learned when we look at true integration and brotherhood which the Prophet ﷺ taught over 1400 years ago. A white-skinned man had no superiority over a black-skinned man but only in terms of piety and righteousness.

Seeking Allāh's ﷻ Pleasure

إِنَّمَا نُطْعِمُكُمْ لِوَجْهِ اللّٰهِ لَا نُرِيدُ مِنْكُمْ جَزَاءً وَّلَا شُكُوْرًا

(Saying) "We feed you only for Allāh's pleasure and desire neither a return nor thanks from you." (76:9)
The Holy Prophet ﷺ said: "I and the guardian of an orphan will be in the Garden (Paradise) like these two," and he held up two fingers close to each other." (Al-Adab ul-Mufrad)

$$\text{إِنَّا نَخَافُ مِنْ رَبِّنَا يَوْمًا عَبُوسًا قَمْطَرِيرًا}$$

Verily we fear from our Lord a Day that will be severe and extremely bitter. (76:10)

The Arabic words, 'A'būsan Qamtarīra' which are used in this verse mean 'extremely bitter'. The word 'A'bas' is used to describe a person who frowns. 'Abus' refers to a person's facial expression and 'Qamtarīra' refers to the frown lines that become impressed on the forehead and face when they express their displeasure.

Allāh ﷻ praises these people; those who do not wish to be recognised for their kindness and compassion but rather, they hope that this will draw the mercy and compassion of their Lord on a Day which will be extremely difficult.

When Sayyidah Ā'ishah ﷺ would give anything to charity, she would send one of her servants and say, "Whatever Du'ā they give, reciprocate it back to the person so that the reward of the Sadaqah remains unaffected."

Nowadays, if we give to a person and they do not thank us or express their gratitude, then we would think twice about giving them anything again, feeling that these people are not worthy on account of their ingratitude. However, Islām teaches us that even expecting this much appreciation is not acceptable. On the other hand, the recipient of the gift is taught to express their gratitude and show their appreciation upon receiving any gift, whether it is substantial, or very small and insignificant.

At the time when the Persian empire was conquered by the Muslims, one of the Sahābah ؓ came with the crown of Rustum and placed it upon the table with all the other jewels that had come into the hands of the Muslims. The people upon seeing this man completely covered and concealed appealed to the man, saying, "Please reveal your identity so that we may see who you are." The person replied, "The One Who I have done this for knows my identity so I do not need to reveal it to anyone."

This was the level of sincerity amongst the Sahābah ؓ to such an extent that to Allāh ﷻ, the Noble Sahābah ؓ giving one date in the path of Allāh ﷻ would be equivalent to us giving a mountain as big as Uhud in gold.

When a person gives a gift to the recipient, they too should try to reciprocate the gift as mentioned in the Hadīth. If they are unable to, then they should make Du'ā until they feel that they have reciprocated the gift even though the person who is giving should not expect any of this.

The pious people will receive all of their blessings fully in Jannah.

فَوَقَاهُمُ اللّٰهُ شَرَّ ذٰلِكَ الْيَوْمِ وَلَقَّاهُمْ نَضْرَةً وَّسُرُوْرًا

So Allāh will save them from the difficulty of that Day and will give them radiance and joy. (76:11)

Before we were sent to this world, when our souls were in the Ālam-e-Arwāh (world of souls), Allāh ﷻ questioned us regarding Himself,

$$\text{وَإِذْ أَخَذَ رَبُّكَ مِنْ بَنِي آدَمَ مِنْ ظُهُورِهِمْ ذُرِّيَّتَهُمْ وَأَشْهَدَهُمْ عَلَىٰ أَنْفُسِهِمْ أَلَسْتُ بِرَبِّكُمْ ۖ قَالُوا بَلَىٰ ۛ شَهِدْنَا ۛ أَنْ تَقُولُوا يَوْمَ الْقِيَامَةِ إِنَّا كُنَّا عَنْ هَٰذَا غَافِلِينَ}$$

When your Lord extracted from the backs (loins) of the children of Ādam their descendants and called them to witness over themselves saying, 'Am I not your Lord?' They replied, 'Certainly! We testify to it.' (This was done) so that you do not say on the Day of Judgement, 'Indeed we were unaware of this.' (7:172)

These were the people who fulfilled this promise, they were the Abrār (righteous).

The Prophet ﷺ said, "There are three whom Allāh ﷻ will not look or praise on the Day of Judgement and for them will be a painful punishment: the one who wears his garments below his ankles, the one who reminds others of his favours, and the one who sells his products by means of making false oaths." (Muslim)

In another Hadīth the Prophet ﷺ said: "Whatever of the Izār (lower garment) is below the ankles is in the Fire." (Bukhāri)

There are those who give, but their donations do not stem from the kindness of their heart but rather; to impress others and to be seen as being charitable. These are the type of people who even though they may give to the poor or help others, they will constantly remind their recipients of how much they have given to them to the point that the recipient of their donation or gift is always left feeling belittled.

Allāh ﷻ says in another verse:

قَوْلٌ مَّعْرُوفٌ وَمَغْفِرَةٌ خَيْرٌ مِّن صَدَقَةٍ يَتْبَعُهَا أَذًى ۗ وَاللَّهُ غَنِيٌّ حَلِيمٌ

A kind word and forgiveness is better than charity followed by hurt. Allāh is Independent, Tolerant. (2:263)

يَا أَيُّهَا الَّذِينَ آمَنُوا لَا تُبْطِلُوا صَدَقَاتِكُم بِالْمَنِّ وَالْأَذَىٰ كَالَّذِي يُنفِقُ مَالَهُ رِئَاءَ النَّاسِ وَلَا يُؤْمِنُ بِاللَّهِ وَالْيَوْمِ الْآخِرِ ۖ فَمَثَلُهُ كَمَثَلِ صَفْوَانٍ عَلَيْهِ تُرَابٌ فَأَصَابَهُ وَابِلٌ فَتَرَكَهُ صَلْدًا ۖ لَّا يَقْدِرُونَ عَلَىٰ شَيْءٍ مِّمَّا كَسَبُوا ۗ وَاللَّهُ لَا يَهْدِي الْقَوْمَ الْكَافِرِينَ

O you who have Īmān! Do not make your charity worthless by reminders of your generosity or by causing hurt (to the recipient) like him who spends his wealth to show people and does not believe in Allāh and the Last Day. His likeness is like that of a smooth rock on which there is some sand. Struck by a rainstorm, it is left bare. They have no control of anything they earn. Allāh does not guide a nation of disbelievers. (2:264)

Sayyidunā Abū Hurairah ؓ reported that the Prophet ﷺ said: "He has not thanked Allāh ﷻ who has not thanked people." (Abū Dāwūd)

The sheer regret that man will feel on that Day when those who disbelieved will be filled with remorse. Allāh ﷻ says:

$$يَقُوْلُ يَالَيْتَنِيْ قَدَّمْتُ لِحَيَاتِيْ$$

He will say, 'Oh dear! If only I had sent good deeds ahead for my life.' (89:24)

$$يَاأَيُّهَا النَّاسُ اتَّقُوا رَبَّكُمْ ۚ إِنَّ زَلْزَلَةَ السَّاعَةِ شَيْءٌ عَظِيْمٌ$$

O people! Fear your Lord. The earthquake of the Day of Judgment is a tremendous thing indeed (22:1)

The Day will be so difficult and severe as Allāh ﷻ says:

$$يَوْمَ تَرَوْنَهَا تَذْهَلُ كُلُّ مُرْضِعَةٍ عَمَّا أَرْضَعَتْ وَتَضَعُ كُلُّ ذَاتِ حَمْلٍ حَمْلَهَا وَتَرَى النَّاسَ سُكَارَى وَمَا هُمْ بِسُكَارَى وَلَٰكِنَّ عَذَابَ اللهِ شَدِيْدٌ$$

When you witness the Day (of Judgement), every nursing mother will forget her suckling infant and every pregnant woman will abort (her unborn child). You will also see people in a drunken stupor although they will not be drunk, but (they will be in this

condition because they will realise that) Allāh's punishment is severe. (22:2)

$$يَوْمَ هُم بَارِزُونَ ۖ لَا يَخْفَىٰ عَلَى اللَّهِ مِنْهُمْ شَيْءٌ ۚ لِّمَنِ الْمُلْكُ الْيَوْمَ ۖ لِلَّهِ الْوَاحِدِ الْقَهَّارِ$$

The Day they will come forward and nothing of theirs will be hidden from Allāh. (On the Day of Judgement, Allāh will announce), 'To whom does all Kingdom belong today?' (He will then reply by saying), 'To Allāh, the One, the Omnipotent.' (40:16)

After Allāh ﷻ asks the question, "To whom does all the Kingdom belong today?" 40 years will pass by where there will be unuttered silence, before Allāh ﷻ will announce, "To Allāh, the One, the Omnipotent."

$$كُلُّ نَفْسٍ ذَائِقَةُ الْمَوْتِ ۗ وَإِنَّمَا تُوَفَّوْنَ أُجُورَكُمْ يَوْمَ الْقِيَامَةِ ۖ فَمَن زُحْزِحَ عَنِ النَّارِ وَأُدْخِلَ الْجَنَّةَ فَقَدْ فَازَ ۗ وَمَا الْحَيَاةُ الدُّنْيَا إِلَّا مَتَاعُ الْغُرُورِ$$

Every soul shall taste death and it is only on the Day of Judgement that you will be given your rewards in full. Whoever is saved from the Fire and entered into Jannah is truly successful. The life of this world is merely an enjoyment of deception. (3:185)

$$وُجُوهٌ يَوْمَئِذٍ نَّاضِرَةٌ ۞ إِلَىٰ رَبِّهَا نَاظِرَةٌ$$

Many faces on that Day will be resplendent looking at their Lord. (75:22–23)

This will be the countenance of the righteous people. However those that will be condemned to the Hellfire will have expressions of despondency etched in their faces.

وَوُجُوهٌ يَوْمَئِذٍ بَاسِرَةٌ ۞ تَظُنُّ أَن يُفْعَلَ بِهَا فَاقِرَةٌ ۞

And many faces on that Day will be gloomy, sensing that they will be dealt with most severely. (75:24–25)

On that Day, people will be in so many different conditions and states. There will be those who will be walking on their hands, upturned because they will not be allowed to stand upright. Others will be transformed into animals such as pigs, apes and monkeys. There will be others who will be drowning in their own sweat. It is only those who are righteous that will be saved from the terrors that will unfold on that frightful Day.

Virtues of Wudhū

When the Prophet ﷺ was asked as to how he would recognise the people of his Ummah, he said that they would have light shining forth from their faces and limbs. This will be due to the effects of performing Wudhū (ablution).

Sayyidunā Abū Hurairah ؓ reported that the Messenger of Allāh ﷺ went to the (Baqi) cemetery and said, "May you be secured from punishment, O dwellers of abode of the believers! We, if Allāh wills, will follow you. I wish we see my brothers." The Companions ؓ said, "Are we not your brothers?" He said, "You are my Companions but my brothers are those who have not come into the world yet." They said, "O Messenger of Allāh ﷺ, how will you recognise those of your Ummah who are not born yet?" He said, "Say, if a man has white-footed horses with white foreheads among horses which are pure black, will he not recognise his own horses?" They said, "Certainly, O Messenger of Allāh ﷺ!" He said, "They (my followers) will come with bright faces and white limbs because of Wudhū and I will arrive at the Hawdh Kawthar ahead of them." (Muslim)

In another Hadīth, Nu'aim Al-Mujmir ؓ narrates, "Once I went up the roof of the Masjid along with Abū Hurairah. He performed ablution and said, "I heard the Prophet ﷺ saying: On the Day of Resurrection, my followers will be called 'Al-Ghurrul-Muhajjalūn from the traces of ablution and whoever can increase the area of his radiance should do so (i.e. by performing ablution regularly)." (Bukhārī)

'Al-Ghurr ul-Muhajjalūn' is the title that will be given on the Day of Resurrection to the Muslims; which means beautiful and radiant. The limbs washed by Muslims during Wudhū will be glistening. This radiance will be one of the unique distinguishing features that will be given to the Ummah of Muhammad ﷺ on the Day of Judgement.

Al-Bazzār narrated from Sayyidunā Abdullāh Ibn Mas'ūd ؓ that the Holy Prophet ﷺ said: "May Allāh beautify a man who hears a saying of mine, then he memorises it and conveys it as he heard it."

This Hadīth contains a supplication of the Holy Prophet ﷺ that a person will be full of radiance who memorises a Hadīth and conveys it in its exact form as he heard it.

Why will the righteous be rewarded? Allāh ﷻ says:

$$وَجَزَاهُمْ بِمَا صَبَرُوا جَنَّةً وَّحَرِيْرًا$$

As a reward for their patience (in this world), they shall have Jannah and (garments and bedding made of the purest) silk. (76:12)

In this world, men are prohibited from wearing silk and gold but in Jannah, there will be no restriction.

$$\text{نَحْنُ أَوْلِيَاؤُكُمْ فِي الْحَيَاةِ الدُّنْيَا وَفِي الْآخِرَةِ ۖ وَلَكُمْ فِيهَا مَا تَشْتَهِي أَنْفُسُكُمْ وَلَكُمْ فِيهَا مَا تَدَّعُونَ}$$

We (angels) were your allies in worldly life and (are so) in the Hereafter. And you will have therein whatever your souls desire, and you will have therein whatever you request (or wish) (41:31)

The reward for patience is indeed great as Allāh ﷻ says:

$$\text{قُلْ يَا عِبَادِ الَّذِينَ آمَنُوا اتَّقُوا رَبَّكُمْ ۚ لِلَّذِينَ أَحْسَنُوا فِي هَذِهِ الدُّنْيَا حَسَنَةٌ ۗ وَأَرْضُ اللَّهِ وَاسِعَةٌ ۗ إِنَّمَا يُوَفَّى الصَّابِرُونَ أَجْرَهُمْ بِغَيْرِ حِسَابٍ}$$

Say, 'O those slaves of Mine who have Īmān! Fear your Lord. There shall be good in this world for those who do good. Allāh's earth is vast. The patient ones shall be granted their reward without reservation.' (39:10)

Categories of Sabr (Patience)

Sabr (patience) is not restricted to cases which entail difficulties, it refers to the other categories of Sabr also. The different categories of Sabr are as follows:

1. Sabr Alal Musībah – having patience after a calamity or a hardship, for example, after a person's loved one passes away.

2. Sabr Alal Itā'at – Sabr upon obedience. This can also be presented in an example: the time for Ishā prayer commences and a person wishes to go out to pray only to realise that it is snowing outside. Despite this, a person still perseveres and goes out to the Masjid to perform the prayer, enduring the hardship that is entailed from the bitter cold weather.

Allāh ﷻ gives glad tidings of a light which will shine forth on the Day of Judgement, for those that came to the Masjid to pray their Salāh.

Sayyidunā Buraydah Al-Aslami ؓ reports that the Prophet ﷺ said: "Give glad tidings to those who walk to the Masjid in darkness of perfect light on the Day of Resurrection." (Abū Dāwūd)

3. Sabr Anil Ma'siah – patience against disobedience. A person for example, passes by a nightclub and has the urge to enter but refrains from going and restrains their Nafs because of the fear of Allāh ﷻ.

4. Sabr - e- Jamīl – the Sabr which is beautiful; without any complaint or ingratitude. When Sayyidunā Ya'qūb ؑ went through the trial of being separated from his son, Sayyidunā Yūsuf ؑ, he displayed this beautiful patience. Allāh ﷻ says:

$$\text{فَصَبْرٌ جَمِيْلٌ ۖ وَاللهُ الْمُسْتَعَانُ عَلٰى مَا تَصِفُوْنَ}$$

"I shall exercise patience without any complaint and I shall seek Allāh's assistance against what you have devised." (12:18)

The word 'Jamīl' (beautiful) has been used in three places in the Qur'ān:

1. Sabr-e-Jamīl – beautiful patience without any complaint as mentioned above.
2. Safha-Jamīl – forgiving someone in a beautiful manner, i.e. when a person forgives a person who has wronged them, they completely erase it from their memory and never bring it up again in reminding a person of what hardship they put them through even when they get angry.
3. Hajre Jamīl – departing from a person in a beautiful manner. For example when a person just cannot get along with someone, they should say Salām and depart and not engage in backbiting or any other form of ill talk about them.

When we are going through hardships in life, we must exercise Sabr and in our times of happiness, we should express our gratitude. Sayyidunā Anas Ibn Mālik ؓ reported that the Messenger of Allāh ﷺ said:
"A time of patience will come upon people in which adhering to one's religion is like grasping a hot coal." (Tirmizī)

Once a husband and wife were sat together and the wife turned to her husband and remarked, "You and me are both in Jannah!" The husband asked in surprise, "How did you come to this conclusion?" The wife replied, "You express your gratitude because you have a beautiful wife like me, and as I have an ugly husband like yourself I am always patient. Allāh ﷻ will reward both those who are patient and grateful with Paradise, hence both of us will go to Paradise!"

Sabr and Shukr (gratitude) are two sides of the same coin. Our state will always exist as one of the two sides.

Bounties of Jannah

مُّتَّكِئِيْنَ فِيْهَا عَلَى الْأَرَائِكِ ۚ لَا يَرَوْنَ فِيْهَا شَمْسًا وَّلَا زَمْهَرِيْرًا

They will recline on couches there and will feel neither (the discomfort of) heat nor (the misery of) cold. (76:13)

In Jannah, everything will be adjusted to perfection so that a person will never suffer from any extreme conditions such as fluctuation in temperature or any other extreme changes in the elements of weather.

وَدَانِيَةً عَلَيْهِمْ ظِلَالُهَا وَذُلِّلَتْ قُطُوْفُهَا تَذْلِيْلًا

Its shade will be close above them and its bunches of fruit will hang low. (76:14)

The shade in Jannah is vast as mentioned in the following Hadīth: Sayyidunā Abū Hurairah ؓ reported Allāh's Messenger ﷺ as saying: "In Paradise, there is a tree under the shadow of which a rider can travel for a hundred years." (Muslim) If this is *just* the shade of a tree, then one can only imagine the size of Jannah that a person will receive.

Allāmah Shabbīr Ahmad Uthmāni ؒ says, "People in Jannah will do Tasbīhāt spontaneously and whenever a person desires something, they will say 'Subhānakallāhumma' and immediately it will be in their presence."

In this world, just as we greet each other by saying Salām, the salutation in Jannah will also be in exchanging the greetings of peace. The Angels will also descend in greeting people by saying Salām.

اَلَّذِيْنَ تَتَوَفَّاهُمُ الْمَلَائِكَةُ طَيِّبِيْنَ ۙ يَقُوْلُوْنَ سَلَامٌ عَلَيْكُمُ ادْخُلُوا الْجَنَّةَ بِمَا كُنْتُمْ تَعْمَلُوْنَ

Those whose souls the Angels claim while they are pure, they (the angels will) say (to them on the Day of Judgement), 'Peace be upon you. Enter Jannah because of the (good) deeds that you performed.' (16:32)

In another verse Allāh ﷻ says:

سَلَامٌ عَلَيْكُمْ بِمَا صَبَرْتُمْ ۚ فَنِعْمَ عُقْبَى الدَّارِ

(The Angels will say) Salām (peace) be upon you for that patience that you exercised (in this world). How blissful is the outcome of the Hereafter! (13:24)

$$سَلَامٌ قَوْلًا مِّنْ رَّبٍّ رَّحِيْمٍ$$

(And) "Peace," a word from a Merciful Lord. (36:58)

$$إِنَّ الْمُتَّقِيْنَ فِيْ مَقَامٍ أَمِيْنٍ ۞ فِيْ جَنَّاتٍ وَّعُيُوْنٍ ۞ يَلْبَسُوْنَ مِنْ سُنْدُسٍ وَّإِسْتَبْرَقٍ مُّتَقَابِلِيْنَ ۞$$

Verily those with Taqwa (God consciousness) shall be in a place of peace in Jannat and springs. They will wear clothing of fine silk and thick silk, and will be seated facing each other. (44:51–53)

Allāh ﷻ will announce to the people of Jannah:

$$يَا عِبَادِ لَا خَوْفٌ عَلَيْكُمُ الْيَوْمَ وَلَا أَنْتُمْ تَحْزَنُوْنَ$$

"O my bondsmen! You shall have no fear today neither will you grieve." (43:68)

Sayyidunā Jabir ؓ reported the Prophet ﷺ saying, "The inhabitants of Jannah will eat and drink therein, but they will not have to pass excrement, blow their noses or urinate. Their food will be digested with belches which will give out a smell like that of musk. They will be inspired to do Tasbīh and proclaim the Greatness of Allāh ﷻ in the same way that they will breathe." (Muslim)

In Jannah, a person will get every type of fruit that their heart will desire, and it will come to them when they desire it, whether they are standing, sitting or lying down. If they wish for the fruits to be peeled, they will be peeled. If they do not wish to use their hands to eat, the food will travel to their mouth without them needing to exert any effort. After eating, there will be no need to relieve oneself, a simple belch will complete digestion. The perspiration which will then emit from a person will be fragrant like musk.

$$وَيُطَافُ عَلَيْهِمْ بِآنِيَةٍ مِّن فِضَّةٍ وَأَكْوَابٍ كَانَتْ قَوَارِيرَا ۝ قَوَارِيرَ مِن فِضَّةٍ قَدَّرُوهَا تَقْدِيرًا ۝$$

Utensils of silver will be brought to them as well as glasses of crystal, such crystal that is of silver with an appropriate measure. (76:15-16)

Even in Jannah, the food will be in the precise measure for a person to consume, not less or more but in the exact and precise proportion without any waste.

$$وَيُسْقَوْنَ فِيهَا كَأْسًا كَانَ مِزَاجُهَا زَنجَبِيلًا ۝ عَيْنًا فِيهَا تُسَمَّىٰ سَلْسَبِيلًا ۝$$

They will be given a drink from cups containing a mixture of ginger. (From) a spring there called Salsabīl. (76:17–18)

The drink that will be given will be Zanjabīl, which will be a mixture of ginger. Even though the names that are used bear resemblance to the names we use to describe the food of this world, the taste will be far more refined and on a whole unique level of its own, so the sensation of all the different flavours cannot even be comprehended. The ginger will have 70 different types of taste. This Zanjabīl comes from the fountain which is called Salsabīl. The word Salsabīl comes from the word 'Salsal', which means flowing because it continuously gushes forth.

Allāh ﷻ says in another verse:

وَبَشِّرِ الَّذِيْنَ آمَنُوْا وَعَمِلُوا الصَّالِحَاتِ أَنَّ لَهُمْ جَنَّاتٍ تَجْرِيْ مِنْ تَحْتِهَا الْأَنْهَارُ ۖ كُلَّمَا رُزِقُوْا مِنْهَا مِنْ ثَمَرَةٍ رِّزْقًا ۙ قَالُوْا هٰذَا الَّذِيْ رُزِقْنَا مِنْ قَبْلُ ۖ وَأُتُوْا بِهٖ مُتَشَابِهًا ۖ وَلَهُمْ فِيْهَا أَزْوَاجٌ مُّطَهَّرَةٌ ۖ وَّهُمْ فِيْهَا خَالِدُوْنَ

And give good news to those who have Īmān and who do good acts that for them shall be gardens beneath which rivers flow. Whenever they are given any fruit to eat there, they will say, 'This is what we were fed with before.' However, the fruit given to them shall only look the same (the taste, smell and other qualities will be very different from the fruits of this world). There they shall have spouses who have been purified and they will live there forever. (2:25)

وَيَطُوفُ عَلَيْهِمْ وِلْدَانٌ مُّخَلَّدُونَ إِذَا رَأَيْتَهُمْ حَسِبْتَهُمْ لُؤْلُؤًا مَّنثُورًا

Lads of eternal youth will wait on them (to serve them whatever they wish). When you see them you will think that they are scattered pearls. (76:19)

Everywhere a person looks, they will see these youths, ready and waiting to serve the people in Jannah. They will remain eternally youthful so they will never grow tired or weary of serving them.

وَإِذَا رَأَيْتَ ثَمَّ رَأَيْتَ نَعِيمًا وَمُلْكًا كَبِيرًا

If you look there, you will see (tremendous) bounties and an enormous kingdom. (76:20)

Sayyidunā Abdullāh ؓ narrates that the Prophet ﷺ said: "I know the person who will be the last to come out of the (Hell) Fire, and the last to enter Paradise. He will be a man who will come out of the Hell (Fire) crawling, and Allāh will say to him, 'Go and enter Paradise.' He will go to it but will imagine that it has been filled, and then he will return and say, 'O Lord, I have found it full.' Allāh will say, 'Go and enter Paradise, and you will have what equals the world and ten times as much (or you will have as much as ten times the like of this world).' On that the man will say, 'Do you mock at me (or laugh at me) though You are the King?' I saw Allāh's Messenger (while saying that) smiling that his premolar teeth became visible. It is said that will be the lowest in degree amongst the people of Paradise." (Bukhāri)

The vision a person will be endowed with will enable them to see the vast range from even a thousand miles away of their kingdom.

عَالِيَهُمْ ثِيَابُ سُندُسٍ خُضْرٌ وَإِسْتَبْرَقٌ ۖ وَحُلُّوٓا۟ أَسَاوِرَ مِن فِضَّةٍ وَسَقَىٰهُمْ رَبُّهُمْ شَرَابًا طَهُورًا

Their clothing will be (made of) fine green silk and thick silk. They will be adorned with bangles of silver and their Lord shall give them pure drinks. (76:21)

The people of Jannah will serve their own drinks as well as be served their drinks and in this verse it states that Allāh ﷻ, their Lord will be serving them drinks. This will be served according to the three different classes:

- As'hābul Yamīn (the people of the right hand) – these will be the righteous people. They will serve themselves.
- Khawās (Elite) - these will be the foremost of the righteous. Angels will serve them.
- Akhas al-Khawās (Special Elite) – these will be foremost of the highest level. Allāh ﷻ will serve them.

The third category of people will be those of the highest level and Allāh ﷻ will Himself directly be giving them their drinks. The reason for these bounties and blessings will be due to the effort of their hard work.

$$\text{إِنَّ هَٰذَا كَانَ لَكُمْ جَزَاءً وَكَانَ سَعْيُكُم مَّشْكُورًا}$$

This is your reward. Your efforts have been appreciated. (76:22)

The smallest of deeds can be appreciated so much by Allāh ﷻ that it can be on the virtue of that deed alone that a person will enter Jannah. For example, the woman who was admitted to Jannah for giving water to a thirsty dog.

The reason a person will be given their reward will be as a result of their endeavour and effort. In another verse Allāh ﷻ says:

$$\text{مَّا يَفْعَلُ اللَّهُ بِعَذَابِكُمْ إِن شَكَرْتُمْ وَآمَنتُمْ ۚ وَكَانَ اللَّهُ شَاكِرًا عَلِيمًا}$$

What would Allāh do with your punishment if you are grateful and believe? Allāh is Most Appreciative, All-Knowing. (4:147)

One of Allāh's ﷻ attributes is that He is Shākir; He is the One who appreciates a person's righteous deeds and actions. Even the smallest of deed that a person does is not left unappreciated by Allāh ﷻ. A special position of distinction are for those who feed the poor, orphan, needy and the captive. The fulfilment of the Huqūqul Ibād (the rights of the servants) is a major part of a person achieving piety and God consciousness.

Even when the Holy Prophet ﷺ first received divine revelation, Sayyidah Khadījah ؓ consoled the Holy Prophet ﷺ when he feared that something had happened to him. She said: "Never! By Allāh. Allāh will never disgrace you. You keep good relations with your kith and kin, help the poor and the destitute, serve your guests generously and assist the calamity-afflicted ones." (Bukhārī)

The Holy Prophet ﷺ said; "Whoever relieves the hardship of a believer in this world, Allāh ﷻ will relieve his hardship on the Day of Resurrection. Whoever helps ease one in difficulty, Allāh ﷻ will make it easy for him in this world and the Hereafter. Whoever conceals the faults of a Muslim, Allāh ﷻ will conceal his faults in this world and in the Hereafter. Allāh ﷻ helps the servant as long as he helps his brother. Whoever travels along the path of knowledge, Allāh ﷻ will make it easy for him a path to Paradise. People do not gather in the Houses of Allāh ﷻ, reciting the Book of Allāh ﷻ and studying it together, but that tranquillity will descend upon them, mercy will cover them, Angels will surround them and Allāh ﷻ will mention them to those near Him. Whoever is slow to good deeds will not be hastened by his lineage." (Muslim)

In another verse, Allāh ﷻ says :

إِنَّ اللهَ يُدْخِلُ الَّذِيْنَ آمَنُوْا وَعَمِلُوا الصَّالِحَاتِ جَنَّاتٍ تَجْرِيْ مِنْ تَحْتِهَا الْأَنْهَارُ يُحَلَّوْنَ فِيْهَا مِنْ أَسَاوِرَ مِنْ ذَهَبٍ وَّلُؤْلُؤًا ۖ وَلِبَاسُهُمْ فِيْهَا حَرِيْرٌ

Allāh will surely admit those who have Īmān and who do good acts into Jannah beneath which rivers flow. There they will be adorned with bangles of gold and pearls. Their clothes in Jannah shall be (made) of silk. (22:23)

Qur'ān Revealed in Stages

إِنَّا نَحْنُ نَزَّلْنَا عَلَيْكَ الْقُرْآنَ تَنْزِيلًا

Verily We have revealed the Qur'ān to you bit by bit. (76:23)

The disbelievers would question why the Qur'ān was not revealed all at once.

وَقَالَ الَّذِينَ كَفَرُوا لَوْلَا نُزِّلَ عَلَيْهِ الْقُرْآنُ جُمْلَةً وَاحِدَةً ۚ كَذَٰلِكَ لِنُثَبِّتَ بِهِ فُؤَادَكَ ۖ وَرَتَّلْنَاهُ تَرْتِيلًا

Those who commit disbelief say, 'Why is the entire Qur'ān not revealed to him all at once?' Thus (it is) so that your heart may be strengthened by it and We have revealed it gradually. (25:32)

The Prophet ﷺ would draw comfort and consolation from the verses as they were revealed, particularly in those moments when he felt that his circumstances were dire due to the abuse and maltreatment the polytheists would cause him. This was also a means of enabling the Qur'ān to be put into practice effectively.

If everything was revealed at once, then even its implementation would have proved challenging as we wouldn't have known what verse to act upon in which order. To incorporate all these practices at once would have proved impossibly difficult. So Allāh ﷻ in His infinite mercy, revealed it in stages so that the commands could be established in succession rather than abruptly. This allowed for the smooth transition of the new commands as they were easily adapted.

Take for example the verses pertaining to the consumption of alcohol. The polytheists made up a nation in which consuming alcohol was part of their social upbringing. If Allāh ﷻ had revealed the verse forbidding the consumption of alcohol abruptly, then few people would have managed to follow it. We see this even in Western society where drinking is commonplace; the powerful effect that it possesses over a person. Those who have an alcohol addiction find it very difficult to give it up and those who manage to do so, spend a great length of time in struggling to wean themselves off its compulsive effects.

Subhān-Allāh – look at Allāh's ﷻ compassion and mercy. Knowing that this would be a difficult struggle for some, Allāh ﷻ in His infinite wisdom, allowed room for the gradual elimination of this vice.

The first verse revealed regarding alcohol to warn people of its dangers, was put subtly in the following verse:

$$\text{وَمِن ثَمَرَاتِ النَّخِيلِ وَالْأَعْنَابِ تَتَّخِذُونَ مِنْهُ سَكَرًا وَرِزْقًا حَسَنًا ۗ إِنَّ فِي ذَٰلِكَ لَآيَةً لِّقَوْمٍ يَعْقِلُونَ}$$

From the fruits of the date palm and vines you make intoxicants (like wine) and good food (such as vinegar and raisins). Indeed there is a sign in this for those who understand. (16:67)

This was the first verse to be revealed that gave a distinct indication that Allāh's ﷻ bounties should not be misspent in producing things that have harmful effects.

$$\text{يَسْأَلُونَكَ عَنِ الْخَمْرِ وَالْمَيْسِرِ ۖ قُلْ فِيهِمَا إِثْمٌ كَبِيرٌ وَمَنَافِعُ لِلنَّاسِ وَإِثْمُهُمَا أَكْبَرُ مِن نَّفْعِهِمَا ۗ وَيَسْأَلُونَكَ مَاذَا يُنفِقُونَ قُلِ الْعَفْوَ ۗ كَذَٰلِكَ يُبَيِّنُ اللَّهُ لَكُمُ الْآيَاتِ لَعَلَّكُمْ تَتَفَكَّرُونَ}$$

They question you about (the permissibility of) liquor and gambling. Say, 'In both is great sin and some benefits for man; but the sin is far greater than their usefulness.' And they ask you what they ought to spend. Say, '(Spend) that which is easy.' In this manner Allāh makes clear to you His revelation so that you may reflect. (2:219)

After this verse was revealed, some of the believers gave up drinking alcohol whilst others felt that as there was no clear-cut prohibition, they could continue consuming it.

It so happened that once during the Maghrib Salāh, the person leading the prayer had drank alcohol and was reciting Sūrah Kāfirūn. Instead of reciting 'Lā A'budu Mā Ta'budūn' (I do not worship what you worship), he recited, 'A'budu Mā Ta'budūn' (I worship what you worship). He had made a great error in his recitation. The Sahābah Kirām ﷺ became perturbed and went to the Prophet ﷺ seeking advice and it was at this moment that the following verse was revealed:

يَا أَيُّهَا الَّذِينَ آمَنُوا لَا تَقْرَبُوا الصَّلَاةَ وَأَنْتُمْ سُكَارَى حَتَّىٰ تَعْلَمُوا مَا تَقُولُونَ وَلَا جُنُبًا إِلَّا عَابِرِي سَبِيلٍ حَتَّىٰ تَغْتَسِلُوا ۚ وَإِنْ كُنْتُمْ مَرْضَىٰ أَوْ عَلَىٰ سَفَرٍ أَوْ جَاءَ أَحَدٌ مِنْكُمْ مِنَ الْغَائِطِ أَوْ لَامَسْتُمُ النِّسَاءَ فَلَمْ تَجِدُوا مَاءً فَتَيَمَّمُوا صَعِيدًا طَيِّبًا فَامْسَحُوا بِوُجُوهِكُمْ وَأَيْدِيكُمْ ۗ إِنَّ اللَّهَ كَانَ عَفُوًّا غَفُورًا

O you who have Īmān! Do not come near Salāh when you are intoxicated until you are (sober and) aware of what you are saying (in your Salah)... (4:43)

After this incident, people gave up drinking during the day. But at night, after Ishā Salāh, they would gather together and drink. It was at this time that one person, in a drunken state, hit another person with the shoulder joint of a camel.

Sayyidunā Abū Maysarah ﷺ said that the verses came after requests by Sayyidunā Umar al-Fārūq ﷺ, "Give us a clear ruling regarding Al-Khamr." (Ahmad)

The following verse was then revealed:

$$\text{يَا أَيُّهَا الَّذِينَ آمَنُوا إِنَّمَا الْخَمْرُ وَالْمَيْسِرُ وَالْأَنْصَابُ وَالْأَزْلَامُ رِجْسٌ مِنْ عَمَلِ الشَّيْطَانِ فَاجْتَنِبُوهُ لَعَلَّكُمْ تُفْلِحُونَ ۞ إِنَّمَا يُرِيدُ الشَّيْطَانُ أَنْ يُوقِعَ بَيْنَكُمُ الْعَدَاوَةَ وَالْبَغْضَاءَ فِي الْخَمْرِ وَالْمَيْسِرِ وَيَصُدَّكُمْ عَنْ ذِكْرِ اللهِ وَعَنِ الصَّلَاةِ ۖ فَهَلْ أَنْتُمْ مُنْتَهُونَ ۞}$$

O you who have Īmān. Indeed liquor, gambling, idols and (distribution by arrows) are filth (vile acts) from the acts of Shaytān. So abstain from them so that you may be successful. Shaytān wants only to cast enmity and hatred between you by means of liquor and gambling and wants to prevent you from the remembrance of Allāh and Salāh. So will you not abstain? (5:90–91)

When this verse was revealed, categorically stating that alcohol was forbidden, those who had taken it into their mouths, at that moment immediately spewed it out. Every last trace of alcohol was removed from their homes; barrels of wine were spilled out and emptied in the streets.

Sayyidunā Abū Sa'īd Al-Khudri ؓ reports that the Prophet ﷺ was addressing people in Madīnah, saying: "O people, Allāh ﷻ is alluding to wine. Perhaps Allāh ﷻ will soon reveal an order regarding it. Whoever has some of it, let him sell it and benefit from it." We did not wait but a little while until the Holy Prophet ﷺ said, "Verily, Allāh ﷻ has forbidden wine. Whoever knows this verse and has some of it, let him neither drink it nor sell it." The people came out into the street with what they had and poured it out. (Muslim)

The following reasons are given as to why alcohol was forbidden:
- It creates enmity.
- It creates hatred.
- It prevents the Dhikr (remembrance) of Allāh ﷻ.
- It prevents a person from performing their Salāh.

Good Company

فَٱصْبِرْ لِحُكْمِ رَبِّكَ وَلَا تُطِعْ مِنْهُمْ آثِمًا أَوْ كَفُورًا

So remain steadfast on the command of your Lord and do not obey any sinner or disbeliever from them. (76:24)

In this verse, 'Āthiman'(sinner) was in reference to Utbah Ibn Rabī'ah as he was an open sinner and transgressor. 'Kafūra' refers to Walīd Ibn Mughīrah. Despite him being in possession of so much wealth, he would turn away the orphans and needy when they came to him in need of help and assistance.

The people whom we befriend also affect the way in which we behave. If we keep the company of those that impact us negatively, then there is a real danger that their vices will permeate into our own manner and mode of behaviour, or mentally constrain us. In order to prevent this, Allāh ﷻ then commanded the Prophet ﷺ to stay clear from these people because of their plotting and conniving.

Sayyidunā Abū Hurairah ؓ reports that the Messenger of Allāh ﷺ said: "A man is upon the religion of his best friend, so let one of you look at whom he befriends." (Tirmizi)

One of the signs of the Day of Judgement is that a person will keep their friends close to them and their parents at a distance. Allāh ﷻ says in the Qur'ān:

$$\text{يَا أَيُّهَا الَّذِيْنَ آمَنُوا اتَّقُوا اللهَ وَكُوْنُوا مَعَ الصَّادِقِيْنَ}$$

O you who have Īmān. Fear Allāh and stay with the truthful. (9:119)

Consultation of the Polytheists

The polytheists gathered together in a meeting to decide how to stop the Prophet ﷺ from further propagating his Message. They felt that one of the ways the Prophet ﷺ was captivating the people's attention was by talking about the bounties and blessings of Jannah. They felt that maybe they could bribe him by offering him wealth and women. They nominated two leaders, Utbah Ibn Rabī'ah and Walīd Ibn Mughīrah, to put forward the following proposal: Utbah Ibn Rabī'ah spoke, saying, "We are all from the same tribe of Quraysh so we are like family. We want to make sure that you are pleased as well as we are happy. We wish to see our community united together so the best thing to do is come to a compromise. I have a very beautiful daughter. I shall wed my daughter to you and give you as much wealth as you desire. In that way you will have everything and you can then forsake speaking ill of our god's and stop talking about the Hūrul-Iyn of Jannah."

Walīd Ibn Mughīrah was the richest man in Makkah. He said to the Prophet ﷺ, "You know that I am a very rich man. My wealth extends from Makkah Mukarramah to Tāif. I have so many orchards and fields producing crops, cattle and slaves. Recently I have started taking out the precious stones from the pits, these have been sent to Egypt and Shām (Syria). The proposal I put forward to you is that I will give you half of my wealth on the condition that you stop talking about the wealth of Paradise."

The Holy Prophet ﷺ could barely believe his ears as to the proposals that the chiefs of Makkah were putting forward. He knew that by refusing such a proposal, his people would taunt and sneer at him for allowing such a prospect to slip through his fingers. On the other hand, if he were to accept such a proposition then he would have been in greater error as the proposal was set with all the wrong conditions, he would not have been able to speak against idol worship.

So, naturally he refused and did not yield into their offers. His mission was far more noble than being succumbed into accepting the transitory glitter and glamour that the worldly temptations had to offer. The Holy Prophet ﷺ did not accept their offers because his mission was to reveal and propagate the Dīn of Allāh ﷻ.

Conveying the Message

$$\text{يَا أَيُّهَا الرَّسُولُ بَلِّغْ مَا أُنْزِلَ إِلَيْكَ مِنْ رَبِّكَ ۖ وَإِنْ لَمْ تَفْعَلْ فَمَا بَلَّغْتَ رِسَالَتَهُ ۚ وَاللَّهُ يَعْصِمُكَ مِنَ النَّاسِ ۗ إِنَّ اللَّهَ لَا يَهْدِي الْقَوْمَ الْكَافِرِينَ}$$

O Prophet! Propagate what has been revealed to you from your Lord. If you do not do so then you have not conveyed Allāh's Message. Allāh shall protect you from the people. Surely Allāh does not guide the nation of disbelievers. (5:67)

In another verse Allāh ﷻ says:

$$\text{إِنَّا نَحْنُ نَزَّلْنَا الذِّكْرَ وَإِنَّا لَهُ لَحَافِظُونَ}$$

Without doubt only We have revealed the Reminder and We shall certainly be its Protectors. (15:9)

The Arabic word 'Nazzalnā' which is used in this verse, refers to revelation that was revealed in stages. This is the reason the Qur'ān was revealed over a period of 22 years, two months and 22 days.

At the time of Shāh Abdul Azīz ﷺ, a Christian priest objected saying that Dhikr (in the above verse) could refer to the Taurāh (Torah) or

Injīl (Bible) because they were revelations which were also sent down. Shāh Abdul Azīz ؒ responded by saying that the word 'Nazzalnā' refers to revelation that was revealed gradually, which will imply to the Holy Qur'ān whereas the Taurāh, Zabūr Injīl were revealed all at once. In another verse Allāh ﷻ says:

$$إِنَّا أَنزَلْنَاهُ فِي لَيْلَةِ الْقَدْرِ$$

Verily We revealed it on the night of Qadr. (97:1)

The Qur'ān was revealed from the Lawh Mahfūz to the first heavens all at once and then from there, it was revealed gradually.

Developing Humility

In a Hadīth, it mentions that those who tend to rear sheep and goats adopt qualities of humility and humbleness, and those who favour breeding horses and camels tend to exhibit prideful qualities. Even the animals we care and tend to have an effect on the way we behave, as mentioned in the following Hadīth:

Sayyidunā Abū Hurairah ؓ reports that the Messenger of Allāh ﷺ said: "The head of disbelief is in the east; pride and arrogance is found in the owners of horses and camels who are rude and uncivil people of tents; and humbleness is found among those who tend to goats or sheep." (Muslim)

The Prophet ﷺ also said: "It is better to sit alone than in company with the bad; and it is better still to sit with the good than alone. It is better to speak to a seeker of knowledge than to remain silent; but silence is better than idle words." (Bukhārī)

Significance of Dhikr

وَاذْكُرِ اسْمَ رَبِّكَ بُكْرَةً وَأَصِيلًا

Remember the name of your Lord morning and evening. (76:25)

This refers to the Dhikr of remembering Allāh's ﷻ Name. This is why when the Sūfis do the Dhikr, they repeat the phrases 'Lā Ilāha Illallāh' (there is no god but Allāh) and 'Allāh, Allāh… Allāh'. The Arabic phrase used here is 'Isma Rabbik' which refers to remembering Allāh's ﷻ Name. In Arabic, the phrase 'morning and evening' is another way of saying all day long.

After we visit the Masjid, our remembrance of Allāh ﷻ should not be left behind at the door of the Masjid but should accompany us throughout our entire day. Islām is not just a religion but a complete way of life. The purpose of our creation is to worship and remember Allāh ﷻ.

When a person exits from the lavatory the first word they are to read is 'Ghufrānak' which means, "(O Allāh) forgive me." Why is a person seeking forgiveness from Allāh ﷻ after coming out of the lavatory? Scholars cite that this is because of the fact that a person was unable to remember Allāh ﷻ in those moments. If this is the case when fulfilling our necessities, then how much more important is it that we use the time we have at our disposal, wisely and not squander.

Even in Jannah, despite a person attaining everything to their hearts content, the only regret the people will have are those moments in which they were not engaged in the remembrance of Allāh ﷻ.

Tahajjud: The Night Prayer

وَمِنَ ٱلَّيۡلِ فَٱسۡجُدۡ لَهُۥ وَسَبِّحۡهُ لَيۡلٗا طَوِيلًا

Prostrate to Him during the night and glorify Him during the long portions of the night. (76:26)

The verse refers to standing up in prayer for part of the night in the Tahajjud prayer.

ٱلَّذِينَ يَذۡكُرُونَ ٱللَّهَ قِيَٰمٗا وَقُعُودٗا وَعَلَىٰ جُنُوبِهِمۡ وَيَتَفَكَّرُونَ فِي خَلۡقِ ٱلسَّمَٰوَٰتِ وَٱلۡأَرۡضِ رَبَّنَا مَا خَلَقۡتَ هَٰذَا بَٰطِلٗا سُبۡحَٰنَكَ فَقِنَا عَذَابَ ٱلنَّارِ

(Those who have intelligence are) they who remember Allāh while standing, sitting and lying down, and they think about the creation of the heavens and earth. (Then amazed by Allāh's crea-

tion they say), 'Our Lord, you have not created all this without a purpose! We glorify Your purity. Save us from the punishment of the Fire.' (3:191)

In another verse Allāh ﷻ says:

$$وَمَا خَلَقْنَا السَّمَاءَ وَالْأَرْضَ وَمَا بَيْنَهُمَا لَاعِبِينَ$$

We have not created the heavens and the earth for idle amusement. (21:16)

The way our pious predecessors would devote themselves to worship leaves us with something extraordinary to marvel at. When Uwais Al-Qarni ؓ for example, stood to perform the Tahajjud prayer he would say, "Tonight is the night of Qiyām," and he would spend his entire night in Qiyām. On other nights he would say, "Tonight is the night of Sajdah," and he would remain in Sajdah all night long.

For 40 years, Imām Abū Hanīfah ؒ performed his Fajr Salāh with the same Wudhū he had used to perform his Ishā Salāh with. Allāhu-Akbar! When the strength of Īmān penetrates a person's heart and firmly implants itself, then seemingly impossible acts become attainable and achievable.

Sayyidunā Hudhaifah ؓ reported: "I offered Salāh (Tahajjud) with the Holy Prophet ﷺ one night and he started reciting Sūrah Al-

Baqarah. I thought that he would bow at the end of 100 verses, but he continued reciting. I then thought that he would perhaps recite the whole Sūrah in a Rak'at but he proceeded on to Sūrah Al-Imrān. He completed it and he then started reciting Sūrah An-Nisā and his recitation was calm. And when he recited the verses which referred to the Glory of Allāh, he glorified Him, the Great, and when he reached the verses that mention supplication, he supplicated, and when he reached the verses that mention seeking refuge of the Lord, He sought (His) refuge. Then he bowed and said, 'Subhāna Rabbiyal Adhīm'; his bowing lasted about the same length of time as his standing (and then returning to the standing posture after Ruku) he said, 'Sami Allāhu Liman Hamida Rabbanā Lakal Hamd'. Then he stood about the same length of time as he had spent in bowing. He then prostrated himself and said, 'Subhāna Rabbiyal A'lā' and his prostration lasted nearly the same length of time as his standing." (Muslim)

Sayyidunā Ibn Mas'ūd ؓ said: "I prayed with Allāh's Messenger ﷺ one night and he stood for so long that I almost resolved to do a very bad thing." When asked what that bad thing was, he said, "I considered sitting down and not continuing to follow the Prophet ﷺ in prayer."

Bukhāri and Muslim narrated from Sayyidunā Abū Salamah Ibn Abdur Rahmān ؓ, that he asked Sayyidah Ā'ishah ؓ: "How did the Messenger of Allāh pray during Ramadhān?" She said, "He did not pray more in Ramadhān or at any other time than 11 Rak'āt. He would pray four Rak'āt, and do not ask how beautiful and long they were. Then he would pray four, and do not ask how beautiful and long they were. Then he would pray three." I said, "O Messenger of Allāh, do you sleep before you pray witr?" He said, "My eyes sleep but my heart does not sleep."

Love of the Dunya

$$\text{إِنَّ هَٰؤُلَاءِ يُحِبُّونَ الْعَاجِلَةَ وَيَذَرُونَ وَرَاءَهُمْ يَوْمًا ثَقِيلًا}$$

Indeed these people love the world and leave behind them a weighty day. (76:27)

When a person has love for the Dunya, the love for the Ākhirah is left far behind. In another place Allāh ﷻ says:

$$\text{كَلَّا بَلْ تُحِبُّونَ الْعَاجِلَةَ ۞ وَتَذَرُونَ الْآخِرَةَ ۞}$$

The fact is that you love this world and you forsake the Hereafter. (75:20-21)

Sayyidunā Ali ؓ would say, "The Dunya and the Ākhirah are like two co-wives. If you make one of them happy, the other will be displeased."

In a Hadīth the Prophet ﷺ said that a person who loves the Dunya would make a loss in the Ākhirah, and the person who loves the

Ākhirah would make a loss in their Dunya, so let him give preference to that which will remain over that which will end.

Once in a gathering, the Prophet ﷺ was mentioning about the Ākhirah and the fire of Jahannam. The Sahābah ؓ were crying upon hearing this but one Sahābi could not cry or even shed a single tear, so he went to the Prophet ﷺ for advice. The Prophet ﷺ said: "The lack of tears is due to hard-heartedness, and the hard-heartedness is because of excessive sinning, and the excessive sinning is due to forgetting death, and a person forgetting death is because of his high expectation in life, and high expectation is because of the love of the Dunya."

The Prophet ﷺ said: "Love of the Dunya is the root of all evil." (Shu'ab ul-Īmān)

The Arabic word 'Yawm' which describes the Day of Judgement has been used in the Holy Qur'ān using many different names. For example; Yawmul Hasrah – the Day of Regret, Yawmut Taghābun – the Day of Winning and Losing and Yawmud Dīn – the Day of Compensation.

Allāh ﷻ says regarding the Day of Judgement:

$$\text{يَا أَيُّهَا النَّاسُ اتَّقُوا رَبَّكُمْ إِنَّ زَلْزَلَةَ السَّاعَةِ شَيْءٌ عَظِيمٌ ۞ يَوْمَ تَرَوْنَهَا تَذْهَلُ كُلُّ مُرْضِعَةٍ عَمَّا أَرْضَعَتْ وَتَضَعُ كُلُّ ذَاتِ حَمْلٍ حَمْلَهَا وَتَرَى النَّاسَ سُكَارَى وَمَا هُم بِسُكَارَى وَلَٰكِنَّ عَذَابَ اللَّهِ شَدِيدٌ ۞}$$

O people! Fear your Lord. The earthquake of the Day of Judgement is a tremendous thing indeed. When you will witness the Day, every nursing mother will forget her suckling infant and every pregnant woman will abort (her unborn child). You will also see people in a drunken stupor although they will not be drunk, but (they will be in this condition because they will realise that) Allāh's punishment is severe. (22:1–2)

$$\text{نَّحْنُ خَلَقْنَاهُمْ وَشَدَدْنَا أَسْرَهُمْ ۖ وَإِذَا شِئْنَا بَدَّلْنَا أَمْثَالَهُمْ تَبْدِيلًا}$$

Only We have created them and only We strengthened their joints and whenever We wish, We could replace them with people just like them. (76:28)

This body of ours sees us through our entire life, mending and repairing itself from within when healing is required, without ourselves needing to service or repair it. The cells regenerate themselves with the body protecting itself from foreign invaders, breakdowns and imbalances.

Sayyidunā Abū Dharr ؓ reports from the Prophet ﷺ, who said: "In the morning, charity is due on every joint in the body of every one of you. Every utterance of Allāh's glorification (i.e. saying Subhān-Allāh) is an act of charity, and every utterance of His praise (i.e. saying Alhamdulillāh) is an act of charity, and every utterance of declaration of His greatness (i.e. saying Lā Ilāha Illallāh) is an act of charity; and enjoining Ma'rūf (good) is an act of charity, and forbidding Munkar (evil) is an act of charity, and two Rak'āt Duhā prayers which one performs in the forenoon is equal to all this (in reward)." (Muslim)

وَاللّٰهُ أَخْرَجَكُم مِّنۢ بُطُونِ أُمَّهَٰتِكُمْ لَا تَعْلَمُونَ شَيْئًا وَجَعَلَ لَكُمُ السَّمْعَ وَالْأَبْصَٰرَ وَالْأَفْـِٔدَةَ ۙ لَعَلَّكُمْ تَشْكُرُونَ

Allāh removed you from the wombs of your mothers when you knew nothing and blessed you with ears, eyes and hearts so that you may be grateful. (16:78)

خَلَقَكُم مِّن نَّفْسٍ وَٰحِدَةٍ ثُمَّ جَعَلَ مِنْهَا زَوْجَهَا وَأَنزَلَ لَكُم مِّنَ الْأَنْعَٰمِ ثَمَٰنِيَةَ أَزْوَٰجٍ ۚ يَخْلُقُكُمْ فِى بُطُونِ أُمَّهَٰتِكُمْ خَلْقًا مِّنۢ بَعْدِ خَلْقٍ فِى ظُلُمَٰتٍ ثَلَٰثٍ ۚ ذَٰلِكُمُ اللّٰهُ رَبُّكُمْ لَهُ الْمُلْكُ ۖ لَا إِلَٰهَ إِلَّا هُوَ ۖ فَأَنَّىٰ تُصْرَفُونَ

He has created you from a single soul, after which He made a spouse from the soul, and also made eight pairs for you from the livestock animals. Allāh creates you in the wombs of your mothers, as a creation after a creation, in three (layers of) darkness. That is Allāh your Lord, to Whom all kingdom belong. There is

none worthy of worship except Him, so where are you turning to? (39:6)

$$\text{يَا أَيُّهَا الْإِنسَانُ مَا غَرَّكَ بِرَبِّكَ الْكَرِيمِ ۞ الَّذِي خَلَقَكَ فَسَوَّاكَ فَعَدَلَكَ ۞ فِي أَيِّ صُورَةٍ مَّا شَاءَ رَكَّبَكَ ۞}$$

O man! What has cast you into deception concerning your Most Generous Lord? Who has created you, perfected (shaped) you, gave you (your body) due proportion and made you in the fashion He desired. (82:6–8)

The beautiful symmetry of design that we see in all animals; if Allāh ﷻ had wished He could have for example, made one arm longer than the other, but He chose symmetry and evenness in the uniformity of each and every type of creation. Although creation, in its resemblance and similarity, share many points of likeness yet, each species is distinctly unique from one another. Mankind is in a class by itself; being the only one of its kind, unlike anything else, excelling every other creation because of man's viable conscience and unparalleled intelligence.

$$\text{إِن يَشَأْ يُذْهِبْكُمْ وَيَأْتِ بِخَلْقٍ جَدِيدٍ ۞ وَمَا ذَٰلِكَ عَلَى اللَّهِ بِعَزِيزٍ ۞}$$

If He wills, He could remove you and replace you with a new creation. That is not at all difficult for Allāh. (35:16–17)

When Islām Enters the Heart

Referring back to the verse when Allāh ﷻ says:

$$نَّحْنُ خَلَقْنَاهُمْ وَشَدَدْنَا أَسْرَهُمْ ۖ وَإِذَا شِئْنَا بَدَّلْنَا أَمْثَالَهُمْ تَبْدِيْلًا$$

Only We have created them and only We strengthened their joints. Whenever We wish, We could replace them with people just like them. (76:28)

Despite the fact that Utbah Ibn Rabī'ah, Abū Jahl and Walīd Ibn Mughīrah were staunch enemies of the Prophet ﷺ who left no stone unturned in their animosity and hatred against him but ironically, their sons became some of the most prominent leaders that society has ever witnessed. Sayyidunā Abū Hudhaifah Ibn Utbah ؓ, Sayyidunā Ikrimah Ibn Abū Jahl ؓ and Sayyidunā Khālid Ibn Walīd ؓ respectively were the sons of the three people mentioned above whom Allāh ﷻ chose to replace.

What provides indirect testimonials of the Holy Qur'ān being the word of Allāh ﷻ is the powerful effect it had on those who understood its words. If we think of the Sahābah ؓ such as Sayyidunā Ikrimah Ibn Abū Jahl ؓ and Sayyidunā Khālid Ibn Walīd ؓ. Despite two decades of enmity against the Prophet ﷺ, their hearts were stirred by the message of truth. In the pre-historic days of Arabia, tribal loyalty was paramount and a person stood by the members of their clan whether or not they were in the right or in error.

Imagine the intensified feelings of hate and animosity Sayyidunā Ikrimah Ibn Abū Jahl ؓ would have felt towards the Holy Prophet ﷺ when he found out that his father had been killed by one of the believers. We can also imagine how much animosity Sayyidunā Ikrimah Ibn Abū Jahl ؓ and Sayyidunā Khālid Ibn Walīd ؓ would have had in their hearts prior to their conversion to Islām, towards the Holy Qur'ān which mentioned the punishment that would be directed at their fathers. After this, they would say to the Companions ؓ, "Does Muhammad expect us to believe in him now after he has revealed verses condemning our fathers. This will never be so."

Regarding those who turn away from the Dīn, Allāh ﷻ says:

يَا أَيُّهَا الَّذِيْنَ آمَنُوْا مَنْ يَّرْتَدَّ مِنْكُمْ عَنْ دِيْنِهِ فَسَوْفَ يَأْتِي اللهُ بِقَوْمٍ يُّحِبُّهُمْ وَيُحِبُّوْنَهٗ أَذِلَّةٍ عَلَى الْمُؤْمِنِيْنَ أَعِزَّةٍ عَلَى الْكَافِرِيْنَ يُجَاهِدُوْنَ فِيْ سَبِيْلِ اللهِ وَلَا يَخَافُوْنَ لَوْمَةَ لَائِمٍ ۚ ذٰلِكَ فَضْلُ اللهِ يُؤْتِيْهِ مَنْ يَّشَاءُ ۚ وَاللهُ وَاسِعٌ عَلِيْمٌ

O you have Īmān! Whoever among you turns away from his religion, then Allāh can soon bring another nation whom He loves and who loves Him; who will be kind towards the believers, stern towards the disbelievers and who will strive in Allāh's way without fearing the criticism of those who criticise. This is the grace of Allāh that He grants to whoever He desires. Allāh (the grace of Allāh) is All-Surrounding, (Allāh is) All-Knowing. (5:54)

Yet the verses infiltrated into the hearts of Sayyidunā Ikrimah Ibn Abū Jahl ؓ and Sayyidunā Khālid Ibn Walīd ؓ, and the truth of the words resonated in their ears despite the fact that it stood against all that they had presupposed. At first they felt that if they were to admit to themselves that it was the truth, then they would dishonour their fathers whom they had helped in fighting against what they had once believed was falsehood.

This would have been a great stigma for the sons to go against their own fathers, as this was totally unheard of in Arab society where a son's loyalty lay with obeying their father. These thoughts would have been turned over in their minds many a times and perhaps was the reason that held them back from accepting Islām for many years, and we see the great length of time which passed before these people came into the fold of Islām; in joining the ranks of the Sahābah Kirām ؓ.

Many a time, the truth may be evident to a person but because admitting to its veracity of truth will have social implications, many choose to turn a blind eye to the calling of their Fitrah (innate nature).

Imagine these people who upon accepting Islām would have been spurned by their community for being disloyal to their fathers' legacies, who were hailed as the greatest leaders to die defending their idols. The difficulty which would have played on their minds before they were able to make that transition to belief, becomes evidently clear. But these men had an inner purity which emanated in dispelling all false notions of disbelief which was able to penetrate through all the falsehood in seeking the light of truth. And in recognition of this, Allāh ﷻ blessed them to become amongst the greatest people to walk the surface of the earth.

The Qur'ān is a Reminder

إِنَّ هٰذِهِ تَذْكِرَةٌ ۖ فَمَنْ شَاءَ اتَّخَذَ إِلٰى رَبِّهِ سَبِيلًا

Indeed, this is certainly advice. So whoever wills should adopt a path towards his Lord. (76:29)

وَالَّذِيْنَ جَاهَدُوْا فِيْنَا لَنَهْدِيَنَّهُمْ سُبُلَنَا ۚ وَإِنَّ اللهَ لَمَعَ الْمُحْسِنِيْنَ

We shall definitely show Our avenues (of guidance and insight) to those who exert themselves in Our cause. Verily, Allāh is certainly with those who do good. (29:69)

وَمَا تَشَاءُوْنَ إِلَّا أَنْ يَّشَاءَ اللهُ ۚ إِنَّ اللهَ كَانَ عَلِيْمًا حَكِيْمًا

You cannot will anything without Allāh's will. Verily Allāh is All-knowing, the Wise. (76:30)

$$\text{وَلَوْ شَاءَ رَبُّكَ لَآمَنَ مَنْ فِي الْأَرْضِ كُلُّهُمْ جَمِيعًا ۚ أَفَأَنْتَ تُكْرِهُ النَّاسَ حَتَّىٰ يَكُونُوا مُؤْمِنِينَ ۞ وَمَا كَانَ لِنَفْسٍ أَنْ تُؤْمِنَ إِلَّا بِإِذْنِ اللَّهِ ۚ وَيَجْعَلُ الرِّجْسَ عَلَى الَّذِينَ لَا يَعْقِلُونَ ۞}$$

If your Lord willed, all those on earth would surely have Īmān. Will you force people until they become believers? No soul can have Īmān without Allāh's order (will and grace). Allāh has set impurity upon those who do not (want to) understand. (10:99–100)

The Concept of Fate

Once a person came to Sayyidunā Ali ؓ and asked, "What is fate?" Sayyidunā Ali ؓ replied, "It is a deep ocean, don't dive into it." The man insisted, so Sayyidunā Ali ؓ replied, "It is a dark road, so don't try to tread on its path." When the man continued on with his requests, Sayyidunā Ali ؓ further replied, "It is a secret of Allāh which is kept hidden from you."

As Muslims, we believe in predestination – whatever good or evil is destined from Allāh ﷻ.

Allāh's ﷻ Mercy

$$يُدْخِلُ مَنْ يَشَاءُ فِي رَحْمَتِهِ ۚ وَالظَّالِمِينَ أَعَدَّ لَهُمْ عَذَابًا أَلِيمًا$$

(31) He enters whoever He wills into His mercy and He has prepared a painful punishment for the oppressors (disbelievers). (76:31)

The disbelievers of the Quraysh used to regard those who were of other races and nationalities with contempt (because they were not from the tribal lineage of the Quraysh). They perceived themselves to be superior and above all people. Yet, Allāh ﷻ chose to accept those such as Sayyidunā Bilāl ؓ from Abyssinia and Sayyidunā Salmān Al-Fārsi ؓ from Persia into His mercy, whereas those who viewed themselves of high birth were regarded as the lowest of the low, with Allāh ﷻ mentioning that He has prepared a bitter punishment for them.

Sayyidah Ā'ishah ؓ reported that the Messenger of Allāh ﷺ said: "Follow the right course, seek nearness to Allāh, and give glad tidings. Verily, none of you will enter Paradise by his deeds alone. They said, 'Not even you O Messenger of Allāh.' He said, 'Not even me, unless Allāh grants me His mercy. Know that the most beloved deed to Allāh is that which is done regularly, even if it is small." (Bukhārī)

When we ask Allāh ﷻ to show us His mercy, we are asking for the following four things:

- Tawfīq-e-Tā'at – the ability to do good deeds. When we sin, the ability to carry out virtuous deeds and actions are taken away.
- Farākh-e- Ma'īshat – expansion of Rizq (sustenance). When a person persists in carrying out evil, their sustenance becomes constricted. When we ask Allāh ﷻ to show us mercy, we ask Allāh ﷻ not to restrict our provisions.
- Be-Hisāb Maghfirat – We seek Allāh's ﷻ forgiveness without taking us to account for our wrongdoings.
- Dukhūl-e-Jannat – entry into Jannah, as the place of mercy is Jannah.

The Sahābah ؓ would feel apprehensive, fearing that they would not get to see the Prophet ﷺ in Jannah owing to the high level he would have attained. They felt that they could not attain such an elevated position, but he reassured them that they would all get to see him. If we wish to be in the companionship of our beloved Prophet ﷺ then we too need to make every moment count. We must utilise the time we have at our disposal, in doing righteous actions and deeds.

Hasan Al-Basri ؓ would say: "You are nothing but a number of days, and whenever a day passes away, a part of you passes away."

For those of us who have allowed our life to slip by and now feel hopeless and despondent in feeling that we have left it too late, all is not lost, for Allāh ﷻ says,

قُلْ يَا عِبَادِيَ الَّذِينَ أَسْرَفُوا عَلَىٰ أَنفُسِهِمْ لَا تَقْنَطُوا مِن رَّحْمَةِ اللَّهِ ۚ إِنَّ اللَّهَ يَغْفِرُ الذُّنُوبَ جَمِيعًا ۚ إِنَّهُ هُوَ الْغَفُورُ الرَّحِيمُ

Say, 'O my bondsmen who have wronged their souls! Never lose hope of Allāh's mercy. Verily, Allāh forgives all sins. Undoubtedly, He is the Most Forgiving, the Most Merciful.' (39:53)

If we turn to Allāh ﷻ in sincere repentance, then our sins will be forgiven and we will be completely cleansed of every evil and wrongdoing. May Allāh ﷻ give us all the Tawfīq to turn to Him in making sincere Tawbah (repentance) and purge us all of our every sin and vice. Āmīn.

Other titles from JKN Publications

Your Questions Answered
An outstanding book written by Shaykh Mufti Saiful Islām. A very comprehensive yet simple Fatāwa book and a source of guidance that reaches out to a wider audience i.e. the English speaking Muslims. The reader will benefit from the various answers to questions based on the Laws of Islām relating to the beliefs of Islām, knowledge, Sunnah, pillars of Islām, marriage, divorce and contemporary issues.

UK RRP: £7.50

Hadeeth for Beginners
A concise Hadeeth book with various Ahādeeth that relate to basic Ibādāh and moral etiquettes in Islām accessible to a wider readership. Each Hadeeth has been presented with the Arabic text, its translation and commentary to enlighten the reader, its meaning and application in day-to-day life.

UK RRP: £3.00

Du'ā for Beginners
This book contains basic Du'ās which every Muslim should recite on a daily basis. Highly recommended to young children and adults studying at Islamic schools and Madrasahs so that one may cherish the beautiful treasure of supplications of our beloved Prophet ﷺ in one's daily life, which will ultimately bring peace and happiness in both worlds, Inshā-Allāh.

UK RRP: £2.00

How well do you know Islām?
An exciting educational book which contains 300 multiple questions and answers to help you increase your knowledge on Islām! Ideal for the whole family, especially children and adult students to learn new knowledge in an enjoyable way and cherish the treasures of knowledge that you will acquire from this book. A very beneficial tool for educational syllabus.

UK RRP: £3.00

Treasures of the Holy Qur'ān
This book entitled "Treasures of the Holy Qur'ān" has been compiled to create a stronger bond between the Holy Qur'ān and the readers. It mentions the different virtues of Sūrahs and verses from the Holy Qur'ān with the hope that the readers will increase their zeal and enthusiasm to recite and inculcate the teachings of the Holy Qur'ān into their daily lives.

UK RRP: £3.00

Marriage - A Complete Solution

Islām regards marriage as a great act of worship. This book has been designed to provide the fundamental teachings and guidelines of all what relates to the marital life in a simplified English language. It encapsulates in a nutshell all the marriage laws mentioned in many of the main reference books in order to facilitate their understanding and implementation.

UK RRP: £5.00

Pearls of Luqmān

This book is a comprehensive commentary of Sūrah Luqmān, written beautifully by Shaykh Mufti Saiful Islām. It offers the reader with an enquiring mind, abundance of advice, guidance, counselling and wisdom.

The reader will be enlightened by many wonderful topics and anecdotes mentioned in this book, which will create a greater understanding of the Holy Qur'ān and its wisdom. The book highlights some of the wise sayings and words of advice Luqmān ﷺ gave to his son.

UK RRP: £3.00

Arabic Grammar for Beginners

This book is a study of Arabic Grammar based on the subject of Nahw (Syntax) in a simplified English format. If a student studies this book thoroughly, he/she will develop a very good foundation in this field, Inshā-Allāh. Many books have been written on this subject in various languages such as Arabic, Persian and Urdu. However, in this day and age there is a growing demand for this subject to be available in English.

UK RRP: £3.00

A Gift to My Youngsters

This treasure filled book, is a collection of Islamic stories, morals and anecdotes from the life of our beloved Prophet ﷺ, his Companions ﷺ and the pious predecessors. The stories and anecdotes are based on moral and ethical values, which the reader will enjoy sharing with their peers, friends, families and loved ones.

"A Gift to My Youngsters" – is a wonderful gift presented to the readers personally, by the author himself, especially with the youngsters in mind. He has carefully selected stories and anecdotes containing beautiful morals, lessons and valuable knowledge and wisdom.

UK RRP: £5.00

Travel Companion

The beauty of this book is that it enables a person on any journey, small or distant or simply at home, to utilise their spare time to read and benefit from an exciting and vast collection of important and interesting Islamic topics and lessons. Written in simple and easy to read text, this book will immensely benefit both the newly interested person in Islām and the inquiring mind of a student expanding upon their existing knowledge. Inspiring reminders from the Holy Qur'ān and the blessed words of our beloved Prophet ﷺ beautifies each topic and will illuminate the heart of the reader.

UK RRP: £5.00

Pearls of Wisdom

Junaid Baghdādī ؓ once said, "Allāh ﷻ strengthens through these Islamic stories the hearts of His friends, as proven from the Qur'anic verse,
"And all that We narrate unto you of the stories of the Messengers, so as to strengthen through it your heart." (11:120)
Mālik Ibn Dinār ؓ stated that such stories are gifts from Paradise. He also emphasised to narrate these stories as much as possible as they are gems and it is possible that an individual might find a truly rare and invaluable gem among them.

UK RRP: £6.00

Inspirations

This book contains a compilation of selected speeches delivered by Shaykh Mufti Saiful Islām on a variety of topics such as the Holy Qur'ān, Nikāh and eating Halāl. Having previously been compiled in separate booklets, it was decided that the transcripts be gathered together in one book for the benefit of the reader. In addition to this, we have included in this book, further speeches which have not yet been printed.

UK RRP: £6.00

Gift to my Sisters

A thought provoking compilation of very interesting articles including real life stories of pious predecessors, imaginative illustrations and much more. All designed to influence and motivate mothers, sisters, wives and daughters towards an ideal Islamic lifestyle. A lifestyle referred to by our Creator, Allāh ﷻ in the Holy Qur'ān as the means to salvation and ultimate success.

UK RRP: £6.00

Gift to my Brothers

A thought provoking compilation of very interesting articles including real life stories of pious predecessors, imaginative illustrations, medical advices on intoxicants and rehabilitation and much more. All designed to influence and motivate fathers, brothers, husbands and sons towards an ideal Islamic lifestyle. A lifestyle referred to by our Creator, Allāh ﷻ in the Holy Qur'ān as the means to salvation and ultimate success.

UK RRP: £5.00

Heroes of Islām

"In the narratives there is certainly a lesson for people of intelligence (understanding)." (12:111)

A fine blend of Islamic personalities who have been recognised for leaving a lasting mark in the hearts and minds of people.

A distinguishing feature of this book is that the author has selected not only some of the most world and historically famous renowned scholars but also these lesser known and a few who have simply left behind a valuable piece of advice to their nearest and dearest.

UK RRP: £5.00

Ask a Mufti (3 volumes)

Muslims in every generation have confronted different kinds of challenges. Inspite of that, Islām produced such luminary Ulamā who confronted and responded to the challenges of their time to guide the Ummah to the straight path. "Ask A Mufti" is a comprehensive three volume fatwa book, based on the Hanafi School, covering a wide range of topics related to every aspect of human life such as belief, ritual worship, life after death and contemporary legal topics related to purity, commercial transaction, marriage, divorce, food, cosmetic, laws pertaining to women, Islamic medical ethics and much more.

UK RRP: £30.00

Should I Follow a Madhab?

Taqleed or following one of the four legal schools is not a new phenomenon. Historically, scholars of great calibre and luminaries, each one being a specialist in his own right, were known to have adhered to one of the four legal schools. It is only in the previous century that a minority group emerged advocating a severe ban on following one of the four major schools.

This book endeavours to address the topic of Taqleed and elucidates its importance and necessity in this day and age. It will also, by the Divine Will of Allāh dispel some of the confusion surrounding this topic.

UK RRP: £5.00

Advice for the Students of Knowledge

Allāh describes divine knowledge in the Holy Qur'ān as a 'Light'. Amongst the qualities of light are purity and guidance. The Holy Prophet has clearly explained this concept in many blessed Ahādeeth and has also taught us many supplications in which we ask for beneficial knowledge.

This book is a golden tool for every sincere student of knowledge wishing to mould his/her character and engrain those correct qualities in order to be worthy of receiving the great gift of Ilm from Allāh.

UK RRP: £3.00

Stories for Children

"Stories for Children" - is a wonderful gift presented to the readers personally by the author himself, especially with the young children in mind. The stories are based on moral and ethical values, which the reader will enjoy sharing with their peers, friends, families and loved ones. The aim is to present to the children stories and incidents which contain moral lessons, in order to reform and correct their lives, according to the Holy Qur'ān and Sunnah.

UK RRP: £5.00

Pearls from My Shaykh

This book contains a collection of pearls and inspirational accounts of the Holy Prophet ﷺ, his noble Companions, pious predecessors and some personal accounts and sayings of our well-known contemporary scholar and spiritual guide, Shaykh Mufti Saiful Islām Sāhib. Each anecdote and narrative of the pious predecessors have been written in the way that was narrated by Mufti Saiful Islām Sāhib in his discourses, drawing the specific lessons he intended from telling the story. The accounts from the life of the Shaykh has been compiled by a particular student based on their own experience and personal observation. **UK RRP: £5.00**

Paradise & Hell

This book is a collection of detailed explanation of Paradise and Hell including the state and conditions of its inhabitants. All the details have been taken from various reliable sources. The purpose of its compilation is for the reader to contemplate and appreciate the innumerable favours, rewards, comfort and unlimited luxuries of Paradise and at the same time take heed from the punishment of Hell. Shaykh Mufti Saiful Islām Sāhib has presented this book in a unique format by including the Tafseer and virtues of Sūrah Ar-Rahmān. **UK RRP: £5.00**

Prayers for Forgiveness

Prayers for Forgiveness' is a short compilation of Du'ās in Arabic with English translation and transliteration. This book can be studied after 'Du'ā for Beginners' or as a separate book. It includes twenty more Du'ās which have not been mentioned in the previous Du'ā book. It also includes a section of Du'ās from the Holy Qur'ān and a section from the Ahādeeth. The book concludes with a section mentioning the Ninety-Nine Names of Allāh ﷻ with its translation and transliteration. **UK RRP: £3.00**

Scattered Pearls

This book is a collection of scattered pearls taken from books, magazines, emails and WhatsApp messages. These pearls will hopefully increase our knowledge, wisdom and make us realise the purpose of life. In this book, Mufti Sāhib has included messages sent to him from scholars, friends and colleagues which will be beneficial and interesting for our readers Inshā-Allāh. **UK RRP: £4.00**

Poems of Wisdom

This book is a collection of poems from those who contributed to the Al-Mumin Magazine in the poems section. The Hadeeth mentions "Indeed some form of poems are full of wisdom." The themes of each poem vary between wittiness, thought provocation, moral lessons, emotional to name but a few. The readers will benefit from this immensely and make them ponder over the outlook of life in general.

UK RRP: £4.00

Horrors of Judgement Day
This book is a detailed and informative commentary of the first three Sūrahs of the last Juz namely; Sūrah Naba, Sūrah Nāzi'āt and Sūrah Abasa. These Sūrahs vividly depict the horrific events and scenes of the Great Day in order to warn mankind the end of this world. These Sūrahs are an essential reminder for us all to instil the fear and concern of the Day of Judgement and to detach ourselves from the worldly pleasures. Reading this book allows us to attain the true realization of this world and provides essential advices of how to gain eternal salvation in the Hereafter.
RRP: £5:00

Spiritual Heart
It is necessary that Muslims always strive to better themselves at all times and to free themselves from the destructive maladies. This book focusses on three main spiritual maladies; pride, anger and evil gazes. It explains its root causes and offers some spiritual cures. Many examples from the lives of the pious predecessors are used for inspiration and encouragement for controlling the above three maladies. It is hoped that the purification process of the heart becomes easy once the underlying roots of the above maladies are clearly understood.   **UK RRP: £5:00**

Hajj & Umrah for Beginners
This book is a step by step guide on Hajj and Umrah for absolute beginners. Many other additional important rulings (Masāil) have been included that will Insha-Allāh prove very useful for our readers. The book also includes some etiquettes of visiting (Ziyārat) of the Holy Prophet's ﷺ blessed Masjid and his Holy Grave.
UK RRP £3:00

Advice for the Spiritual Travellers
This book contains essential guidelines for a spiritual Murīd to gain some familiarity of the science of Tasawwuf. It explains the meaning and aims of Tasawwuf, some understanding around the concept of the soul, and general guidelines for a spiritual Murīd. This is highly recommended book and it is hoped that it gains wider readership among those Murīds who are basically new to the science of Tasawwuf.
UK RRP £3:00

Don't Worry Be Happy
This book is a compilation of sayings and earnest pieces of advice that have been gathered directly from my respected teacher Shaykh Mufti Saiful Islām Sāhib. The book consists of many valuable enlightenments including how to deal with challenges of life, promoting unity, practicing good manners, being optimistic and many other valuable advices. Our respected Shaykh has gathered this Naseehah from meditating, contemplating, analysing and searching for the gems within Qur'anic verses, Ahādeeth and teachings of our Pious Predecessors. **UK RRP £1:00**

Kanzul Bāri

Kanzul Bāri provides a detailed commentary of the Ahādeeth contained in Saheeh al-Bukhāri. The commentary includes Imām Bukhāri's biography, the status of his book, spiritual advice, inspirational accounts along with academic discussions related to Fiqh, its application and differences of opinion. Moreover, it answers objections arising in one's mind about certain Ahādeeth. Inquisitive students of Hadeeth will find this commentary a very useful reference book in the final year of their Ālim course for gaining a deeper understanding of the science of Hadeeth.   **UK RRP: £15.00**

How to Become a Friend of Allāh

The friends of Allāh have been described in detail in the Holy Qur'ān and Āhadeeth. This book endeavours its readers to help create a bond with Allāh in attaining His friendship as He is the sole Creator of all material and immaterial things. It is only through Allāh's friendship, an individual will achieve happiness in this life and the Hereafter, hence eliminate worries, sadness, depression, anxiety and misery of this world.   **UK RRP:**

Gems & Jewels

This book contains a selection of articles which have been gathered for the benefit of the readers covering a variety of topics on various aspects of daily life. It offers precious advice and anecdotes that contain moral lessons. The advice captivates its readers and will extend the narrowness of their thoughts to deep reflection, wisdom and appreciation of the purpose of our existence.   **UK RRP: £4.00**

End of Time

This book is a comprehensive explanation of the three Sūrahs of Juzz Amma; Sūrah Takweer, Sūrah Infitār and Sūrah Mutaffifeen. This book is a continuation from the previous book of the same author, 'Horrors of Judgement Day'. The three Sūrahs vividly sketch out the scene of the Day of Judgement and describe the state of both the inmates of Jannah and Jahannam. Mufti Saiful Islām Sāhib provides an easy but comprehensive commentary of the three Sūrahs facilitating its understanding for the readers whilst capturing the horrific scene of the ending of the world and the conditions of mankind on that horrific Day.   **UK RRP: £5.00**

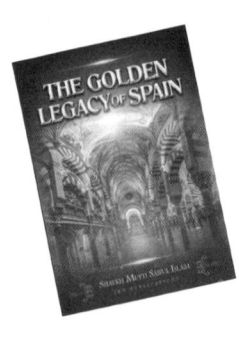

Andalus (modern day Spain), the long lost history, was once a country that produced many great calibre of Muslim scholars comprising of Mufassirūn, Muhaddithūn, Fuqahā, judges, scientists, philosophers, surgeons, to name but a few. The Muslims conquered Andalus in 711 AD and ruled over it for eight-hundred years. This was known as the era of Muslim glory. Many non-Muslim Europeans during that time travelled to Spain to study under Muslim scholars. The remanences of the Muslim rule in Spain are manifested through their universities, magnificent palaces and Masājid carved with Arabic writings, standing even until today. In this book, Shaykh Mufti Saiful Islām shares some of his valuable experiences he witnessed during his journey to Spain.   **UK RRP: £3.00**

Ideal Youth
This book contains articles gathered from various social media avenues; magazines, emails, WhatsApp and telegram messages that provide useful tips of advice for those who have the zeal to learn and consider changing their negative habits and behavior and become better Muslims to set a positive trend for the next generation. **UK RRP:£4:00**

Ideal Teacher
This book contains abundance of precious advices for the Ulamā who are in the teaching profession. It serves to present Islamic ethical principles of teaching and to remind every teacher of their moral duties towards their students. This book will Inshā-Allāh prove to be beneficial for newly graduates and scholars wanting to utilize their knowledge through teaching. **UK RRP:£4:00**

Ideal Student
This book is a guide for all students of knowledge in achieving the excellent qualities of becoming an ideal student. It contains precious advices, anecdotes of our pious predecessors and tips in developing good morals as a student. Good morals is vital for seeking knowledge. A must for all students if they want to develop their Islamic Knowledge. **UK RRP:£4:00**

Ideal Parents
This book contains a wealth of knowledge in achieving the qualities of becoming ideal parents. It contains precious advices, anecdotes of our pious predecessors and tips in developing good parenthood skills. Good morals is vital for seeking knowledge. A must for all parents. **UK RRP:£4:00**

Ideal Couple
This book is a compilation of inspiring stories and articles containing useful tips and life skills for every couple. Marriage life is a big responsibility and success in marriage is only possible if the couple know what it means to be an ideal couple. **UK RRP:£4:00**

Ideal Role Model
This book is a compilation of sayings and accounts of our pious predecessors. The purpose of this book is so we can learn from our pious predecessors the purpose of this life and how to attain closer to the Creator. Those people who inspires us attaining closeness to our Creator are our true role models. A must everyone to read. **UK RRP:£4:00**

Bangladesh– A Land of Natural Beauty
This book is a compilation of our respected Shaykh's journeys to Bangladesh including visits to famous Madāris and Masājid around the country. The Shaykh shares some of his thought provoking experiences and his personal visits with great scholars in Bangladesh.
UK RRP: £4.00

Pearls from the Qur'an
This series begins with the small Sūrahs from 30th Juzz initially, unravelling its heavenly gems, precious advices and anecdotes worthy of personal reflection. It will most definitely benefit both those new to as well as advanced students of the science of Tafsīr. The purpose is to make it easily accessible for the general public in understanding the meaning of the Holy Qur'ān. **UK RRP: £10.00**

When the Heavens Split
This book contains the commentary of four Sūrahs from Juzz Amma namely; Sūrah Inshiqāq, Sūrah Burūj, Sūrah Tāriq and Sūrah A'lā. The first two Sūrahs contain a common theme of capturing the scenes and events of the Last Day and how this world will come to an end. However, all four Sūrahs mentioned, have a connection of the journey of humanity, reflection on nature, how nature changes and most importantly, giving severe warnings to mankind about the punishments and exhorting them to prepare for the Hereafter through good deeds and refraining from sins.
UK RRP: £4.00

The Lady who Spoke the Qur'ān
The Holy Prophet ﷺ was sent as a role model who was the physical form of the Holy Qur'ān. Following the ways of the Holy Prophet ﷺ in every second of our lives is pivotal for success. This booklet tells us the way to gain this success. It also includes an inspirational incident of an amazing lady who only spoke from the Holy Qur'an throughout her life. We will leave it to our readers to marvel at her intelligence, knowledge and piety expressed in this breath-taking episode.
UK RRP:£3:00

Dearest Act to Allāh
Today our Masājid have lofty structures, engraved brickworks, exquisite chandeliers and laid rugs, but they are spiritually deprived due to the reason that the Masājid are used for social purposes including backbiting and futile talk rather than the performance of Salāh, Qur'ān recitation and the spreading of true authentic Islamic knowledge. This book elaborates on the etiquettes of the Masjid and the importance of Salāh with Quranic and prophetic proofs along with some useful anecdotes to emphasize their importance. **UK RRP:£3:00**

Don't Delay Your Nikāh
Marriage plays an important role in our lives. It is a commemoration of the union of two strangers who will spend the rest of their remaining lives with one another. Marriage ought to transpire comfort and tranquillity whereby the couple share one another's sorrow and happiness. It is strongly recommended that our brothers and sisters read and benefit from this book and try to implement it into our daily lives in order to once more revive the Sunnah of the Holy Prophet ﷺ on such occasions and repel the prevalent sins and baseless customs.
UK RRP:£3:00

Miracle of the Holy Qur'ān
The scholars of Islām are trying to wake us all up, however, we are busy dreaming of the present world and have forgotten our real destination. Shaykh Mufti Saiful Islām Sāhib has been conducted Tafsīr of the Holy Qur'ān every week for almost two decades with the purpose of reviving its teachings and importance. This book is a transcription of two titles; Miracle of the Holy Qur'ān and The Revelation of the Holy Qur'ān, both delivered during the weekly Tafsīr sessions.
UK RRP:£3:00

You are what you Eat
Eating Halāl and earning a lawful income plays a vital role in the acceptance of all our Ibādāt (worship) and good deeds. Mufti Saiful Islām Sāhib has presented a discourse on this matter in one of his talks. I found the discourse to be very beneficial, informative and enlightening on the subject of Halāl and Harām that clarifies its importance and status in Islām. I strongly recommend my Muslim brothers and sisters to read this treatise and to study it thoroughly.
UK RRP:£3:00

Sleepers of the Cave

The Tafsīr of Sūrah Kahf is of crucial importance in this unique and challenging time we are currently living in. This book is evidently beneficial for all Muslims, more crucial for the general public. This is because Mufti Sāhib gives us extensive advice on how to act accordingly when treading the path of seeking knowledge. Readers will find amazing pieces of advice in terms of etiquettes regarding seeking knowledge and motivation, Inshā-Allāh. **UK RRP:£5:00**

Contentment of the Heart

The purification of the soul and its rectification are matters of vital importance which were brought by our Holy Prophet e to this Ummah. The literal meaning of Tazkiyah is 'to cleanse'. The genuine Sūfis assert that the foundation and core of all virtuous character is sincerity and the basis for all evil characteristics and traits is love for this world. This book endeavors to address certain spiritual maladies and how to overcome them using Islamic principles. **UK RRP:£5:00**

Contemporary Fiqh

This book is a selection of detailed *Fiqhi* (juridical) articles on contemporary legal issues. These detailed articles provide an in depth and elaborative response to some of the queries posted to us in our Fatawa department over the last decade. The topics discussed range between purity, domestic issues, Halāl and Harām, Islamic medical ethics, marital issues, rituals and so forth. Many of the juristic cases are unprecedented as a result of the ongoing societal changes and newly arising issues. **UK RRP:£6:00**

Ideal Society

In this book, 'Ideal Society' which is a commentary of Sūrah Hujurāt, Shaykh Mufti Saiful Islām Sāhib explains the lofty status of our beloved Prophet ﷺ, the duties of the believers and general mankind and how to live a harmonious social life, which is free from evil, jealousy and vices. Inshā-Allāh, this book will enable and encourage the readers to adopt a social life which will ultimately bring happiness and joy to each and every individual.

UK RRP:£5:00